Mark Ravenhill

Plays: 1

Shopping and Fucking, Faust is Dead, Handbag, Some Explicit Polaroids

Mark Ravenhill's first full-length play *Shopping and Fucking*, produced by Out of Joint and the Royal Court Theatre, opened at the Royal Court Theatre Upstairs in September 1996 and was followed by a national tour. It transferred to the Queen's Theatre in the West End in June 1997 and was followed by an international tour. His second play *Faust is Dead* was produced by Actors' Touring Company (national tour) in 1997. *Sleeping Around*, a joint venture with three other writers, opened at the Salisbury Playhouse in February 1998 before a run at the Donmar Warehouse, London, followed by a national tour. *Handbag* was produced by Actors' Touring Company in 1998. *Some Explicit Polaroids*, for Out of Joint, opened at the Theatre Royal, Bury St Edmunds, followed by a run at the New Ambassadors, London, in October 1999. All the plays have been widely translated and produced across the world.

MARK RAVENHILL

Plays: 1

Shopping and Fucking
Faust is Dead
Handbag
Some Explicit Polaroids

Introduced by Dan Rebellato

Methuen Drama

METHUEN CONTEMPORARY DRAMATISTS

7 9 10 8 6

This collection first published in Great Britain in 2001 by
Methuen Publishing Limited
11–12 Buckingham Gate, London SW1E 6LB

Methuen Publishing Limited Reg. No. 3543167

A CIP catalogue record for this book is available from the British Library

ISBN 10: 0 413 76060 X
ISBN 13: 978 0 413 76060 9

Typeset by SX Composing DTP, Rayleigh, Essex
Printed and bound in Great Britain by
Cox and Wyman Ltd, Reading, Berkshire

Contents

Mark Ravenhill
A Chronology

September 1996	*Shopping and Fucking*, Out of Joint and Royal Court Theatre (Royal Court Theatre Upstairs and national tour)
April 1997	*Faust is Dead*, Actors' Touring Company (Lyric Hammersmith Studio and national tour)
September 1998	*Handbag*, Actors' Touring Company (Lyric Hammersmith Studio and national tour)
September 1999	*Some Explicit Polaroids*, Out of Joint (New Ambassadors Theatre and national tour)

Introduction

In February 2000, as the Royal Court prepared to open their newly refurbished theatre in Sloane Square, the press reported a problem with the computer system. The settings on the internal network, designed to inhibit the sending of obscene or abusive e-mails, was preventing anyone mentioning the name of one of the Court's most successful plays of the 1990s: Mark Ravenhill's *Shopping and Fucking*.

The story reminds us of the persistently disruptive nature of a play whose title could not be displayed outside theatres, printed in full in newspapers or on book covers, nor spoken unprompted on the telephone. Ravenhill is very good at titles, and this one has entered the public consciousness in a way that no play has done perhaps since *Look Back in Anger* forty years before. No doubt it contributed to the international success of this play: two West End runs, a national and international tour, and dozens of other productions around the world.

Along the way, as the play transferred into larger and larger theatres, some of the subtlety of the play might have got trampled down by its 'scandalous' reputation. There was, undoubtedly, a thrill in seeing this defiantly young, queer, strutting play occupy three West End theatres. There's a genuinely contemporary ease in these plays' smart cultural references, rubbing playwrights like Crimp and Brecht up against *The Lion King* and Take That (who lend their names to the protagonists of *Shopping and Fucking*). All of these plays move in a recognisable world of webcams, mobiles, CCTV, and pagers, powered onward in a kind of amyl nitrate rush. But while we should never underplay the genuine originality of the characters, their casually nihilistic amorality, their tracing of new forms of friendship, our developing interactions with information technology, overstating all this cyberglamour distorts the delicate moral shapes of Ravenhill's work, his relationship to traditions of British playwriting that he engages and contests, and the fierce satirical energy that powers the work.

He has a reputation among some critics as a theatrical *enfant terrible* purveying sexually explicit, sensationalist, shock-loaded drama, and there's stuff in the plays one could point to, but Ravenhill is profoundly moral in his portraiture of contemporary society. His vision is elliptically but recognisably social, even socialist. He addresses not the fragments but the whole, offering us not just some explicit polaroids but the bigger picture.

An earlier generation of playwrights developed the 'state-of-the-nation play' as a vehicle to carry their critique of society's political drift. This form – epic in its scope, national in its sweep, often spanning decades – is dying, despite Michael Billington's best efforts. And it's not hard to see why. There seems now something curiously parochial about addressing oneself to a nation at a time when the boundaries of the nation state are being punctured and dismantled by global forces, where one can communicate instantly across continents, where multinational companies do not so much court politicians as shop globally for the cheapest politics they can buy. In the plays gathered here, it seems to me, globalisation is Ravenhill's theme, and he is concerned to trace what happened when we turned from a nation of shopkeepers into a nation of shoppers. It lies only a little below the surface of *Shopping and Fucking*, colours and animates the lives of *Faust is Dead* and *Handbag*, and comes right to the fore in *Some Explicit Polaroids*, in which Jonathan, the George Soros-like international speculator, starkly describes the ecstasy of powerlessness, of individuals swept along by the movements of international capital. Ravenhill shows us our society, the state of our communal bonds, ripped and tattered by transcontinental economic forces. When Microsoft and Monsanto have a firmer grip on our lives than any government agency, the sources of real power seem terrifyingly unreachable and uncontrollable. Small wonder that Nadia in *Some Explicit Polaroids* sees herself as 'alone in the universe'.

In this sense, the uncompromising sexual abundance of the plays is only part of the story. These plays are not just about fucking, but crucially about shopping too. These two terms couple promiscuously through the first play. In the phone sex lines, a topless audition for a shopping channel, rent boys, the variations on a tale of sexual slavery, the terms combine and recombine orgiastically. Yet this is not celebrated. Again and again, the play asks how these activities came to overlap so consistently, whether there is anything left in our lives together that cannot be bought and sold. Tellingly, it is a moment of pure giving – Robbie's distribution of 300 free Es – that gives him a fleeting, chemically-induced rush of global insight. Imagining himself rising above the world and looking down, he declares: 'Fuck it. This selling. This buying. This system. Fuck the bitching world and let's be . . . beautiful. Beautiful. And happy.'

The steady dismantling of those social arrangements which might once have fostered our desire and ability to live together have left these characters without the common bonds to help them do so. Their primary relationships are with consumer goods, and they seem barely able to form any kind of connection with one another. Like the individual microwave meals that Lulu, Mark and Robbie eat, there is no sharing in these characters' lives. They seem to make avoidance of personal contact a badge of pride, like David and Suzanne, the market researchers in *Handbag*, who live with the consumers they are surveying, but stay 'Strictly impersonal. Observation not relationship orientated.' Instead of reaching out to one another – which Mark in *Shopping and Fucking* sees as a dangerous addiction and Victor in *Some Explicit Polaroids* sees as weak – they have turned inwards, gazing emptily at themselves. A mist of pop psychology and vacuous new agery tries to validate this failure to make contact. In *Some Explicit Polaroids*, this narcissistic blather is brilliantly pastiched: 'I can say it now. I'm a nice person. But that's quite a new thing for me, you know?' confesses Nadia. 'We had to practise. With a mirror.'

Inventing characters just to scorn them would make for rather thin entertainment, and there is much more to these plays than that. Unlike Tim in *Some Explicit Polaroids* who patronisingly explains away Nick's early-eighties politics but

xii Mark Ravenhill Plays

remains oblivious to the modishness of his own beliefs, Ravenhill carefully shows us that this preening self-obsession is the exemplary attitude of the world these characters have grown up into. Mark, in *Shopping and Fucking*, only feels comfortable with sex when he has paid for it, when fucking is a form of shopping. Gary, the rent boy, describes Mark's sexual desire for 'the usual things' as 'regular' as if sex were an item on a McDonald's menu. And look how Nadia and Tim, in *Some Explicit Polaroids*, describe what they mean by 'being happy':

Tim   It means we're content with what we've got.
Nadia   And we're at peace with ourselves.
Tim   And we take responsibility for ourselves.
Nadia   And we're our own people.
Tim   And we're not letting the world get to us.

The avalanche of triteness is hilariously well-observed. In particular the phrase 'we're our own people' hangs around in these plays and subtly suggests that economic ownership has come to characterise even the way that we view ourselves. In *Handbag*, Phil is sucking off David, whose pager beeps, announcing that his child is being born. 'Be your own person,' urges Phil, and the ties of kinship and friendship are once again severed by the urge to claim private ownership of your life.

This is what sharply differentiates these plays from the wave of gay plays which preceded *Shopping and Fucking* into the West End. While the feelgood pleasure of Jonathan Harvey's *Beautiful Thing* or the elaborate earnestness of Kevin Elyot's *My Night With Reg* may have paved the way for Ravenhill's plays, he goes far beyond them. As Naomi Klein suggests in her anti-globalisation handbook, *No Logo*, the drift towards identity politics of the 1980s may have played into the hands of corporate power. Campaigning for better representation of marginalised groups was very appealing to sectors of the advertising industry, while a recognition of diversity was easily transformed into a form of niche marketing. It's an arresting and challenging idea, and should be taken seriously for all its abrasiveness. In these plays Ravenhill suggests that an obsession with self is what happened to politics after being processed through an advertiser's focus group. The sexual explicitness in these plays is part of his scandalised portrait of an apolitical generation with no values but economic ones, media-fixated and self-obsessed, fucking while Rome burns.

In Britain, over the last twenty years, the welfare state and all other aspects of civil society – all those institutions that lie between us and corporate power, protecting us from them – have been steadily eroded. But, as these plays show, the desire for protection has not disappeared. Gary in *Shopping and Fucking* and Phil in *Handbag* both cry out for someone to watch over me. In these plays though, it becomes clear that we are now only watched over by CCTV, and even this is largely in the hands of big business (whenever there's a major crime, it's striking that the best quality video images are always from in-store security cameras).

One of the ways that the Conservative governments from 1979 to 1997 habitually undermined the welfare state ideal was by dismissing it as wrong-headed 'paternalism'. The disappearance of this paternalism shows up codedly in many plays of the 1990s in the form of the absent, failing or abusive fathers, notably in David Greig's *The Architect*, Jez Butterworth's *Mojo* and Sarah Kane's *Blasted*, in which fathers are either threatening and dangerous figures, or are absent altogether. Ravenhill's work has a complex and difficult relationship with fathers, who are variously abusing, absent, sugar daddies, roles adopted for daddy/son sexual role play, and even appear in absurdly mythopoeic form in references to *The Lion King*. Characters like Gary and Phil long for fathers, but are denied them. Gary reaches his lowest point when realising that the protecting father he yearns for can never be found: 'he's not out there,' he cries. 'I'm sick and I'm never going to be well.'

In the place of these good fathers step tyrannical violent fathers. Brian weeps watching a video of his son playing the cello, but replaces it in the machine with images of a failed employee being brutally tortured. It's Brian who gives us the key to understanding this strange shift. He asks Robbie what he thinks lies behind all that is good in the world, and receives the hesitant answer, 'a father'. No, he says, it's money. By tearing down the shields protecting us from the gusts and eddies of international finance, we are left at the mercy of larger forces, far more distant from us, hugely more powerful than us. The father that could have saved us has stepped aside, and we are left facing the father who will crush us. This perhaps suggests why, in *Faust is Dead*, Pete's violent absent father is flirtatiously suggested to be the cyberpatriarch Bill Gates.

The Canadian novelist Douglas Coupland is the nearest writer in attitude and tone to Ravenhill, and his *Generation X* is undoubtedly a major influence on *Shopping and Fucking*. In the book, Coupland's rootless young men and women tell each other stories to make sense of their world. As Claire says, 'Either our lives becomes stories, or there's just no way to get through them.' Similarly, in *Shopping and Fucking*, Robbie declares, 'I think we all need stories, we make up stories so that we can get by.' In *Generation X* the narratives they tell each other are referred to as 'bedtime stories', and again we feel the traces of the missing father, whose lack the characters have to fill themselves.

Robbie goes on to suggest that 'a long time ago there were big stories. Stories so big you could live your whole life in them. The Powerful Hands of the Gods and Fate. The Journey to Enlightenment. The March of Socialism. But they all died or the world grew up or grew senile or forgot them, so now we're all making up our own stories. Little stories.' It did not escape the notice of critics that this is a fairly accurate summary of Jean-François Lyotard's *The Postmodern Condition*, nor that Alain in *Faust is Dead* is an amalgam of the French philosophers Michel Foucault and Jean Baudrillard. Alain claims the death of man, the death of the real, the death of progress, all recognisable postmodern slogans.

But we should not let ourselves be dazzled by self-congratulation for spotting these references to the doyens of postmodernist thought, if in doing so we blind ourselves to the fact that Ravenhill's use of their ideas is fiercely sceptical. As we move into the twenty-first century and the habit of claiming the death of things is itself dying, it is easier to see to these proclamations as springing directly from the political cultures in which they were formed. Robbie's speech about stories has a certain weight and seriousness, both in its phrasing and the space made for it in the play, but we should pause before believing Ravenhill has jumped with both feet on to this particular bandwagon. The breathtaking abdication of responsibility that these ideas entail is pointed up sharply in *Faust is Dead*, when Alain discourses with the utmost seriousness about the death of reality, while Donny lies at his feet, really dying. This is emphasised in the revised version published here, in which Donny, who in the first version was just an image on a video screen, was brought physically on to the stage. Ravenhill comically captures a Baudrillardian portentousness when he has Alain declare that reality has been replaced by simulation, bathetically adding that this happened at 'fifteen hundred hours on the thirteenth of August 1987'.

The claim that there are only mini-stories that we carry around with us, that reality has ended, that progress has been discredited, of course, makes resistance to the grand story of globalisation impossible. It makes our experience of reality impossible to share; we move, once again, from members of a common society, to individual consumers of individual story-portions. Ravenhill's characters recite these post-modern platitudes, insisting that nothing should ever mean anything, that truth is no more valuable than lies, that we should never think of the big picture. One cannot understand globalisation without an ability to see beyond oneself to a wider story in which we are all characters; but in *Some Explicit Polaroids*, Tim anxiously tries to prevent knowledge of the world moving beyond the individual: 'Nothing's a pattern unless you make it a pattern. Patterns are only there for people who see patterns, and people who see patterns repeat patterns.' Such thought leaves us entirely defenceless, because it suggests that by changing our minds we change the world. As an unfashionable German thinker from the nineteenth century argued, this is like urging a drowning man to abandon his belief in gravity. Postmodernism, with its refusal to accept that reality is something we share, is the Thatcherite philosophy par excellence. It is the privatisation of public knowledge.

And just as they seek out those idealised fathers, real experiences and real contact are urgently sought by Ravenhill's characters. Against Gary's euphoric version of the future in which we will all communicate through screens and keyboards, looking at holograms of each other – though note that he mistakenly uses the rather more personal word 'holograph', meaning 'signature' – Mark explains that he picked Gary because 'I liked your voice'. Later, Gary's desire for a father is ultimately deeply self-destructive, and similarly Pete's search for real experiences, in *Faust is Dead*, leads him to cut himself. This was no doubt inspired in part by Richey Edwards of the Manic Street Preachers, who in May 1991, while being interviewed by a sceptical journalist, tried to demonstrate the band's authenticity by cutting the words '4 Real' into his forearm. Similar acts are employed theatrically by performance artists like Ron Athey, or Franko B whose blood-letting frequently takes him to the edge of consciousness in his performances, seeking, it seems, the same zeal for authenticity when he insists that 'it's not theatre, you know, it's not fake blood'.

Horrific acts of this kind perhaps suggest that cutting is a desperate way of making contact with reality, pain stimulating a body numbed by the delirium of consumer pseudo-choice and mediation on every level. In *Faust is Dead*, Pete is so alienated from the world and his body that he does not even feel his own orgasm and can only comfortably understand the world when looking at it through the viewfinder of his camcorder. Imagining the money he'll make selling the stolen software, Chaos, back to his father, Pete's vision of freedom is a long and absurd list of real experiences he will buy.

Ravenhill is, both in the plays and in interviews, attracted by the playfulness of paradoxes, and he frequently employs the ironies that they engender. But by this I don't mean the irony whose dead hand has lain so heavily on British culture in the nineties, the ironic kitsch of retro fashion, the ironic reclamations of bad films and minor television personalities. These trends use irony to avoid being committed to anything, lending out alibis against the embarrassment of meaning what we say. Ravenhill's irony is pointed, angry. It recalls the pitiless irony of Bret Easton Ellis, whose *American Psycho* viciously satirised the ethics of Wall Street in the eighties, and *Glamorama* which scours the vacuous celebrity worship of the nineties. Some think these plays alienatingly cool, but it's the coolness of a steely gaze opening up to us the absurdity of so much that passes for wisdom in a consumerist, post-Thatcherite world. What is more, he offers us ways of experiencing an alternative.

Seeing alternatives to what is, imagining what might be, is always difficult and particularly so when people become accustomed to looking inwards for answers, scorning attempts to look out at society or at history. In Douglas Coupland's *Girlfriend in a Coma*, the eponymous Karen lapses into her coma in 1979 and wakes in 1997. A similar device is used in *Some Explicit Polaroids*, where Nick has just been released from prison after fifteen years for kidnapping and torturing a financier. What he finds is the world we have described, intellectually woozy, morally vacant, in which all human relations are economically driven, where a woman who once sought to tear down the system now campaigns to reorganise the local bus timetable. And everywhere there is a sad reiteration of the idea that we have 'grown up'. Helen, the former activist turned New Labour councillor, repudiates a radical pamphlet she wrote some years before; its author was 'Another person,' she says. 'It was a child.' Yet the experience of moving out from under the wing of paternal authority is not uncomplicatedly happy. Later she admits that the drift away from socialism has meant that 'I've cut bits out of myself. Bit by bit, another belief, another dream. I've cut them all out. I'm changed. I've grown up. I'm scarred.' The abandonment of conviction is again experienced intensely in the body, and adulthood means individualism. As Lorraine says in *Handbag*, 'You grow up and you're alone. You gotta do things by yourself.'

But Nick has not grown up. Like the food Nadia finds in the

back of her freezer, stamped 'best before December 1984', he has remained frozen in time. The play was in part inspired by Ernst Toller's *Hoppla! Such is Life!* (1927) in which Karl Thomas is released from a mental hospital eight years after being imprisoned for his role in the 1919 Spartacist uprising in Germany. Like Karl Thomas, Nick serves to ask us what has changed, how our values have evolved, what hopes were realised and which have been neglected. As an outsider who has remained untouched by the social changes that took place between 1984 and 1999, Nick's role in the play is as a human framing device, throwing into relief the absurdities of the present, checking them against a now forgotten alternative.

It gives *Some Explicit Polaroids* an emotional and political urgency that roots the irony in a passionate commitment to social values. No one should mistake the anger that tears through the play. When Jonathan shows Nadia the scars from his torture at the hands of Nick, she offers to 'kiss it better'. Jonathan's response, 'Don't be so fucking stupid. That's not going to work, is it?', is searingly inelegant, clumsy in the mouth, and all the more wrenchingly dramatic for it. For despite his characters' desire to be their own people, their attempt to refuse meaning, to glory in the escape from moral responsibility, reality, and each other, everywhere in the work Ravenhill affirms our fundamentally social character, that we are only ourselves when we are with others, forming human, social bonds that are not driven by economic exchange. Mark is forced to admit to Gary that 'Now, here, when you're with me I feel like a person and if you're not with me I feel less like a person.' Even Nadia, speaking to the dead body of her friend, admits 'I'm alone. That's what I've always been scared of. Being on my own'. Towards the end of *Some Explicit Polaroids* former kidnapper and prisoner, Nick and Jonathan, confront each other. In one of the great scenes of the 1990s, they discover a kinship in their shared recognition that they are part of the same pattern, even if on opposite sides. As Jonathan offers Nick use of his shower, a curious sensuousness curls on to the stage, as if their bodies have found a nostalgic equilibrium in their mutual understanding. Similarly, at the end of *Shopping and Fucking*, the ruthless solo consumerism is broken down as the three friends feed each other from their individual ready-made meals. And, for such a reputedly unsentimental and hard-nosed play, there is a surprising amount of crying, a tear perhaps being, as Brian suggests, 'a drop of pure emotion'.

In such moments, the characters achieve a fleeting insight into their lives, glimpsing, however briefly, a pattern in the chaos. This is beautifully caught early in *Shopping and Fucking* as Lulu auditions for Brian with Irina's speech from the end of Chekhov's *Three Sisters*: 'One day people will know what all this was for. All this suffering. There'll be no more mysteries. But until then we have to carry on living. We must work. That's all we can do'. The speech tears a stylistic hole in the fabric of the play (like the lines from Rilke in *Generation X*). But of course Lulu is acting; does she even understand the significance of the words she is speaking? Indeed, the hundred-year-old speech is making a prediction which Ravenhill's play itself rebuts. Yet the hope, the promise of explanation, is allowed to hang ghostlike in the moment.

Such phantoms and spectres haunt Ravenhill's work, emphasising and underlining our need to be members of a society, our profound yearnings for each other. Despite the characters' rejection of meaning, meanings circulate through these plays, generated between characters, between bodies in space. There are patterns and parallels that reverberate across each play – I've picked out several of them here – echoing those moments where characters are forced to admit their need for one another. The elements of the plays are drawn together just like the characters, almost despite themselves. And as even Brian in *Shopping and Fucking* affirms, it is this sense of beauty, of artistic form, that gives us a glimpse of this alternative way of being: 'you feel it – like something you knew. Something so beautiful that you've lost but you'd forgotten that you've lost it.'

So while the steady erosion of our common lives is demonstrated in these plays, they also affirm what needs to be preserved. It's this sense of affirmation that I would invite the reader to look for in these plays, because few modern plays come burdened with such notoriety as *Shopping and Fucking*.

Critics were unanimous in praising the contemporaneity of these plays, their ability to 'tap into the zeitgeist', and called Ravenhill the playwright of the E-generation. But he speaks to this generation, not necessarily for them. A passionate concern for lives torn and broken by the decline of our collective sensibility animates the work, and there's an arc that leads us from *Shopping and Fucking*, through the personal and philosophical focus of *Faust is Dead* and *Handbag*, to the ambition and scope of *Some Explicit Polaroids*. His next play, *Mother Clap's Molly House*, seems likely to signal a change of direction, but these plays form a coherent and searing body of work in themselves. They offer unexpectedly big stories that lay out the landscape of our changing world, affirming what must be preserved and what, if we are to survive, must be changed.

Dan Rebellato
March 2001

Shopping and Fucking

Shopping and Fucking was first performed at the Royal Court Theatre Upstairs, London, on 26 September 1996. The cast was as follows:

Lulu	Kate Ashfield
Robbie	Andrew Clover
Mark	James Kennedy
Gary	Antony Ryding
Brian	Robin Soans

Directed by Max Stafford-Clark
Designed by Julian McGowan
Lighting by Johanna Town
Sound by Paul Arditti

A slash in the dialogue (/) indicates that the next actor should start their line, creating overlapping speech.

Scene One

Flat – once rather stylish, now almost entirely stripped bare.

Lulu *and* **Robbie** *are trying to get* **Mark** *to eat from a carton of takeaway food.*

Lulu   Come on. Try some.

Pause.

Come on. You must eat.

Pause.

Look, please. It's delicious. Isn't that right?

Robbie   That's right.

Lulu   We've all got to eat.
Here.
Come on, come on.
A bit for me.

Mark *vomits*

Robbie   Shit. Shit.

Lulu   Why does that alw . . . ?
Darling – could you? Let's clean this mess up.
Why does this happen?

Mark   Please.

Lulu   This will . . . come on . . . it's alright.

Mark   Look, please.

Lulu   Thank you.
See? It's going. Going . . . going . . . gone.

Robbie   Alright? OK?

Lulu   Yes, yes. He's alright now.

Mark   Look . . . you two go to bed.

Lulu   Leave you like this?

Mark   I want to be alone for a while.

Robbie   Is someone coming round?

Lulu   Do you owe money?

Mark   No. No one's coming round. Now – go to bed.

Lulu   So what are you going to do?

Mark   Just sit here. Sit and think. My head's a mess. I'm fucked.

Robbie   You'll be alright.

Mark   I'm so tired.
Look at me. I can't control anything. My . . . guts. My mind.

Robbie   We have good times don't we?

Mark   Of course we have. I'm not saying that.

Robbie   Good times. The three of us. Parties. Falling into taxis, out of taxis. Bed.

Mark   That was years ago. That was the past.

Lulu   And you said: I love you both and I want to look after you for ever.

Mark   Look I . . .

Lulu   Tell us the shopping story.

Mark   Please I want to . . .

Robbie   Yeah, come on. You still remember the shopping story.

Pause.

Mark   Well alright.
I'm watching you shopping.

Lulu   No. Start at the beginning.

Mark   That's where it starts.

Robbie No it doesn't. It starts with: 'summer'.

Mark Yes. OK.
It's summer. I'm in a supermarket. It's hot and I'm sweaty.
Damp. And I'm watching this couple shopping. I'm
watching you. And you're both smiling. You see me and you
know sort of straight away that I'm going to have you. You
know you don't have a choice. No control. Now this guy
comes up to me. He's a fat man. Fat and hair and lycra and
he says:
See the pair by the yoghurt?
Well, says fat guy, they're both mine. I own them. I own
them but I don't want them – because you know something?
– they're trash. Trash and I hate them. Wanna buy them?
How much?
Piece of trash like them. Let's say . . . twenty. Yeah, yours
for twenty.
So, I d the deal. I hand it over. And I fetch you. I don't have
to say anything because you know. You've seen the
transaction.
And I take you both away and I take you to my house. And
you see the house and when you see the house you know it.
You understand? You know this place.
And I've been keeping a room for you and I take you into
this room. And there's food. And it's warm. And we live out
our days fat and content and happy.

Pause.

Listen. I didn't want to say this. But I have to.
I'm going.

Lulu Scag. Loves the scag.

Mark Not any more.

Robbie Loves the scag more than he loves us.

Mark Look. Look now. That isn't fair. I hate the scag.

Lulu Still buying the scag though, aren't you?

Mark   No. I'm off the scag. Ten days without the scag. And I'm going away.

Robbie   From us?

Mark   Yes. Tonight.

Lulu   Where are you going?

Mark   I want to get myself sorted. I need help. Someone has to sort me out.

Robbie   Don't do that. You don't need to do that. We're helping you.

Lulu   We're sorting you out.

Mark   It's not enough. I need something more.

Robbie   You're going? And leaving us?

Mark   I'm going to get help.

Robbie   Haven't we tried? We've tried. What do you think we've been doing? All this time. With the . . . clearing up when you, you . . .

Lulu   Where?

Mark   Just a place.

Lulu   Tell us.

Mark   A centre. For treatment.

Lulu   Are you coming back?

Mark   Of course I am.

Robbie   When?

Mark   Well that all depends on how well I respond. To the treatment. A few months.

Robbie   Where is it? We'll visit.

Mark   No.

Robbie   We'll come and see you.

Mark   I mustn't see you.

Robbie   I thought you loved me. You don't love me.

Mark   Don't say that. That's a silly thing to say.

Lulu   Hey. Hey, look. If you're going, then go.

Robbie   You don't love me.

Lulu   Look what you've done. Look what you've done to him.
What are you waiting for? A taxi? Maybe you want me to call a taxi? Or maybe you haven't got the money? You going to ask me for the money? Or maybe just take the money? You've sold everything. You've stolen.

Mark   Yes. It's not working. That's why I'm going.

Lulu   Yes. I think you should. No. Because we're going to be fine. We're going to do very well. And I think maybe you shouldn't come back. We won't want you back.

Mark   Let's wait and see.

Lulu   You don't own us. We exist. We're people. We can get by. Go.
Fuck right off. Go. GO.

Mark   Goodbye.

Exit **Mark**.

Robbie   Stop him. Tell him to stay. Tell him I love him.

Lulu   He's gone now. Come on. He's gone. We'll be alright. We don't need him. We'll get by.

Scene Two

Interview room.

Brian *and* **Lulu** *sit facing each other.* **Brian** *is showing* **Lulu** *an illustrated plastic plate.*

Brian   And there's this moment. This really terrific moment. Quite possibly the best moment. Because really, you see, his father is dead. Yes? The Lion King was crushed – you feel the sorrow welling up in you – crushed by a wild herd of these big cows. One moment, lord of all he surveys. And then . . . a breeze, a wind, the stamping of a hundred feet and he's gone. Only it wasn't an accident. Somebody had a plan. You see?

Lulu   Yes. I see.

Brian   Any questions. Any uncertainties. You just ask.

Lulu   Of course.

Brian   Because I want you to follow.

Lulu   Absolutely.

Brian   So then we're . . . there's . . .

Lulu   Crushed by a herd of wild cows.

Brian   Crushed by a herd of wild cows. Yes.

Lulu   Only it wasn't an accident.

Brian   Good. Excellent. Exactly. It wasn't an accident. It may have looked like an accident but. No. It was arranged by the uncle. Because –

Lulu   Because he wanted to be King all along.

Brian   Thought you said you hadn't seen it.

Lulu   I haven't.
Instinct. I have good instincts. That's one of my qualities. I'm an instinctive person.

Brian   Is that right?

Brian *writes down 'instinctive' on a pad.*

Brian   Good. Instinctive. Could be useful.

Lulu   Although of course I can also use my rational side. Where appropriate.

Brian   So you'd say you appreciate order?

Lulu   Order. Oh yes. Absolutely. Everything in its place.

Brian *writes down 'appreciates order'.*

Brian   Good. So now the father is dead. Murdered. It was the uncle. And the son has grown up. And you know – he looks like the dad. Just like him. And this sort of monkey thing comes to him. And this monkey says: 'It's time to speak to your dead dad.' So he goes to the stream and he looks in and he sees –

Lulu   / His own reflection.

Brian   his own reflection. You've never seen this?

Lulu   Never.

Brian   But then . . . The water ripples, it hazes. Until he sees a ghost. A ghost or a memory looking up at him. His . . .

Pause.

Excuse me. It takes you right here. Your throat tightens. Until . . . he sees . . . his . . . dad.
My little one. Gets to that bit and I look round and he's got these big tears in his eyes. He feels it like I do.
Because now the dad speaks. And he says: 'The time has come. It is time for you to take your place in the Cycle of Being (words to that effect). You are my son and the one true King.'
And he knows what it is he's got to do. He knows who it is he has to kill.
And that's the moment. That's our favourite bit.

Lulu   I can see that. Yes.

Brian   Would you say you in any way resembled your father?

Lulu   No. Not really. Not much.

Brian   Your mother?

Lulu   Maybe. Sometimes. Yes.

Brian   You do know who your parents are?

Lulu   Of course. We still . . . you know. Christmas. We spend Christmas together. On the whole.

Brian *writes down 'celebrates Christmas'.*

Brian   So many today are lost. Isn't that so?

Lulu   I think that's right. Yes.

Brian   And some come here. They look to me. You're looking to me, aren't you?
Well, aren't you?

Lulu   Yes. I'm looking to you.

Brian (*proffers plate*)   Here. Hold it. Just hold it up beside you. See if you look right. Smile. Look interested. Because this is special. You wouldn't want to part with this. Can you give me that look?

Lulu *attempts the look.*

Brian   That's good. Very good. Our viewers, they have to believe that what we hold up to them is special. For the right sum – life is easier, richer, more fulfilling. And you have to believe that too. Do you think you can do that?

Again **Lulu** *attempts the look.*

Brian   Good. That's very good. We don't get many in your league.

Lulu   Really?

Brian   No. That really is very . . . distinctive.

Lulu   Well. Thank you. Thanks.

Brian   And now: 'Just a few more left. So dial this number now.'

Lulu   Just a few more left. So dial this number now.

Brian   Excellent. Natural. Professional. Excellent.

Lulu   I have had training.

Brian   So you're . . . ?

Lulu   I'm, a trained actress.

Brian *writes down 'trained actress'*.

Brian   I don't recognize you.

Lulu   No? Well, probably not.

Brian   Do some for me now.

Lulu   You want me to . . . ?

Brian   I want to see you doing some acting.

Lulu   I didn't realise. I haven't prepared.

Brian   Come on. You're an actress. You must be able to do some acting.
An actress – if she can't do acting when she's asked then what is she?
She's nothing.

Lulu   Alright.

She stands up.

I haven't actually done this one before. In front of anyone.

Brian   Never mind. You're doing it now.

Lulu   One day people will know what all this was for. All this suffering.

Brian   Take your jacket off.

Lulu   I'm sorry?

Brian   I'm asking you to take your jacket off. Can't act with your jacket on.

Lulu   Actually, I find it helps.

Brian   In what way?

Lulu   The character.

Brian   Yes. But it's not helping me. I'm here to assess your talents and you're standing there acting in a jacket.

Lulu   I'd like to keep it on.

Brian (*stands*)   Alright. I'll call the girl. Or maybe you remember the way.

Lulu   No.

Brian   What do you mean – no?

Lulu   I mean . . . please I'd like this job. I want to be considered for this job.

Brian   Then we'll continue. Without the jacket. Yes?

Lulu *removes her jacket. Two chilled ready meals fall to the floor.*

Brian   Look at all this.

They both go to pick up the meals. **Brian** *gets there first.*

Exotic.

Lulu   We've got really into them. That's what we eat. For supper.

Brian   Did you pay for these?

Lulu   Yes.

Brian   Stuffed into your jacket. Did you pay for them?

Lulu   Yes.

Brian   Look me in the eyes. Did. You. Pay?

Lulu   No.

Brian   Stolen goods.

Lulu   We have to eat. We have to get by. I don't like this. I'm not a shoplifter. By nature. My instinct is for work. I need a job. Please.

Brian   You're an actress by instinct but theft is a necessity. Unless you can persuade me that I need you.
Alright. Carry on. Act a bit more.
No shirt.

Lulu   No . . .

Brian   Carry on without the . . . (what's the . . . ?) . . . blouse. And the . . .

Lulu *removes her blouse.*

Lulu   One day people will know what all this was for. All this suffering. There'll be no more mysteries. But until then we have to carry on living. We must work. That's all we can do. I'm leaving by myself tomorrow . . .

Brian (*stifling a sob*)   Oh God.

Lulu   I'm sorry. Shall I stop?

Brian   Carry on. Please.

Lulu   I'm leaving by myself tomorrow. I'll teach in a school and devote my whole life to people who need it. It's autumn now. It will soon be winter and there'll be snow everywhere. But I'll be working.
That's all.

Lulu *puts her blouse and jacket on.*

Brian (*wipes away a tear*)   Perfect. Brilliant. Did you make it up?

Lulu   No. I learnt it. From a book.

Brian   Brilliant. So you think you can sell?

Lulu   I know I can sell.

Brian   Because you're an actress?

Lulu   It helps.

Brian   You seem very confident.

Lulu   I am.

Brian   Alright then. A trial. Something by way of a test. I'm going to give you something to sell and we're going to see how well you do. Clear so far?

Lulu   Totally.

Lulu   Yes.

Brian   You understand that I am *entrusting* you?

Lulu   I understand.

Brian   I am entrusting you to pass this important test.

Lulu   I'm not going to let you down.

Brian *reaches for his briefcase and starts to open it.*

Scene Three

Flat.

Robbie *is sitting. He is wearing the uniform of a leading burger chain.* **Lulu** *stands over him.*

Robbie   And all I've said was: With cheese, sir?
And he just looks at me blankly. Just stares into my eyes.
And there's this . . . fear.
Try again. 'Would you like cheese on your burger, sir?'
This is too much for him. I see the bottom lip go. The eyes are filling up.

Lulu   So you told him. And they sacked you?

Robbie   Someone had to. If you were there you'd . . . I decided I'm going to have to tell him. And I say: Look, here you have a choice. For once in your life you have a choice so for fuck's sake make the most of it.

Lulu   And then they / sacked you?

Robbie   And then. He gets his fork. Grabs this fork. And he jumps over the counter. And he goes for me.

Lulu   With the fork?

Robbie   Goes for me with the fork. Gets me down and stabs me.

Lulu   He stabbed you?

Beat.

Robbie   It's nothing.

Lulu   You're wounded. You should have told me.

Robbie   No. It's nothing.

Lulu   Where's the wound then?

Robbie   It snapped. Before it did any damage.

Lulu   ?

Robbie   The fork. It was a plastic fork. It snapped before it did any damage.

Pause.

Lulu   So . . . no wound? So. Where's the money going to come from? Who's gonna pay for everything?

Robbie   You'll come up with something.

Lulu   Me?

Robbie   Yeah. You'll sort it out.
Did you get it?

Lulu   Did I get . . . ?

Robbie   The job. The TV.

Lulu   Well. Yes. They're taking me on . . .

Robbie   Brilliant. / That's brilliant.

Lulu   They're offering me a sort of temporary assignment.

Robbie   Yeah? What sort of . . . ?

Lulu *produces three hundred E in a clear plastic bag.*

Robbie   You're gonna sell them?

Lulu   We're going to sell them. You can make yourself useful.
Should be three hundred. You can count them.

Exit **Lulu**. **Robbie** *starts counting the tablets.* **Mark** *enters and watches* **Robbie**, *who doesn't see him until –*

Mark   Are you dealing?

Robbie   Fuck. You made me –
How long have you – ?

Mark   Just now. Are you dealing?

Robbie   That doesn't . . .

Pause.

So. They let you out.

Mark   Sort of.

Pause.

Robbie   Thought you said months. Did you miss me?

Mark   I missed you both.

Robbie   I missed you. So. I s'pose . . .
I sort of hoped you'd miss me.

Mark   Yeah. Right.

Robbie *moves to* **Mark**. *They kiss.*

Robbie *moves to kiss* **Mark** *again.*

Mark   No.

Robbie   No?

Mark   Sorry.

Robbie   No. That's OK.

Mark No, sorry. I mean it. Because actually I'd decided I wasn't going to do that. I didn't really want that to happen, you know? Commit myself so quickly to . . . intimacy.

Robbie OK.

Mark Just something I'm trying to work through.

Robbie . . . Work through?

Mark Yeah. Sort out. In my head.
We've been talking a lot about dependencies. Things you get dependent on.

Robbie Smack.

Mark Smack, yes absolutely. But also people. You get dependent on people. Like . . . emotional dependencies. Which are just as addictive, OK?

Robbie (*pause*) So – that's it, is it?

Mark No.

Robbie That's me finished.

Mark No.

Robbie 'Goodbye.'

Mark I didn't say that. No. Not goodbye.

Robbie Then . . . kiss me.

Mark Look . . . (*Turns away.*)

Robbie Fuck off.

Mark Until I've worked this through.

Pause.

Robbie Did you use?

Mark No.

Robbie Right. You used, they chucked you out.

Mark Nothing. I'm clean.

Robbie So . . .

Pause.

Mark There are these rules, you see. They make you sign
– you agree to this set of rules. One of which I broke.
OK?

Robbie Which one?

Mark It was nothing.

Robbie Come on.

Mark I told them. It wasn't like that. I put my case /
but –

Robbie *Tell me.*

Pause.

Mark No personal relations.

Robbie Fuck.

Mark You're not supposed to – form an attachment.

Robbie Ah, I see.

Mark Which I didn't.

Robbie So that's why / you won't kiss me.

Mark It wasn't an attachment.

Robbie (*pause*) If you were just honest. / We said we'd be
honest.

Mark It wasn't like that. I told them 'You can't call this a
personal relationship.'

Robbie What was it then?

Mark More of a . . . transaction. I paid him. I gave him
money. And when you're paying, you can't call that a
personal relationship, can you? / What would you call it?

Robbie   You can't kiss me. You fucked someone / but you can't kiss me.

Mark   That would mean something.

Robbie   Who was it?

Mark   Somebody.

Robbie   Tell me who.

Mark   He was called Wayne.

Robbie   Well get you.

Mark   I just – you know – in the shower. Shower and I . . . Saw his bottom. Saw the hole, you know. And I felt like – I wanted to . . . lick it.

Robbie (*pause*)   That's it?

Mark   We did a deal. I paid him. We confined ourselves to the lavatory. It didn't mean anything.

Robbie   Nothing for afters?

Mark   That's all.

Robbie   Just Lick and Go.

Mark   It wasn't a personal relation.

Robbie (*lets trousers drop*)   Well, if you can't kiss my mouth.

Mark   No. With you – there's . . . baggage.

Robbie   Well, excuse me. I'll just have to grow out of it.

Robbie *pulls his trousers up. Pause.*

Mark   I'm sorry.

Robbie   Sorry? No. It's not . . . sorry doesn't work. Sorry's not good enough.

Pause.

Mark   You're dealing?

Robbie   Doesn't matter.

Mark   Thought so.

Robbie   Listen, this stuff is happiness. Little moment of heaven. And if I'm spreading a little – no a great big fuck off load of happiness –

Pause. **Robbie** *picks up an E between thumb and forefinger.*

Mark   It's not real.

Robbie   Listen, if you, if this, this . . . planet is real . . .

He takes an E. Pause.

Waiting for you. Do you know what it's like – waiting? Looking forward to this day – for you to . . . And you – Oh fuck it. Fuck it all.

Robbie *takes another E.*

Enter **Lulu** *with two microwaved ready meals on a tray.*

Lulu   I . . . They let you out. It's sooner . . .

Mark   Yeah. They let me out. Thought I'd come back. See if you're alright.

Pause.

Lulu   I've only got enough for two.

Mark   Never mind.

Lulu   It's just hard to share them. They're done individually.

Mark   Oh well.

Lulu   Well . . . hello.

Mark   Hello.

Lulu   We've got really into the little boxes with the whole thing in it. One each.

Robbie Looks great, doesn't she?
Gonna be on TV, aren't you?

Lulu They're . . . considering it. It's just a / little . . .

Robbie Just she says. Only. It's TV.

Mark Great.

Robbie You see, we're doing something? Aren't we?

Lulu Yes.

Robbie We're working. Providing.

Mark So will I. Yes. I'll sort myself out and we'll be OK.

Lulu They're really not made for sharing. It's difficult.

Mark It's OK. I'll go out.

Robbie Back to Wayne?

Mark No. Out. Find some food. Shopping.

Robbie Don't just – don't stand there and judge us.

Mark Cheeseburger. Some chocolate maybe.

Robbie I want you to be part of this.

Mark I've hurt you. I see that. But – please just let me . . .
I've got to take this a step at a time, OK?

Exit **Mark**.

Robbie Cunt. Cunt. / Cunt.

Lulu I know, I know.

Robbie Hate the cunt.

Lulu That's it. Come on. / Come on.

Robbie Hate him now.

Lulu Yes. Yes. Yes.

Robbie I want him to suffer.

Pause.

Lulu   Did you count them?

Robbie   Oh. Yes. Yesyesyes.

Lulu   And was it? Three hundred. Exactly.

Robbie   Yes. Three hundred. Exactly.

Scene Four

A bedsit.

Gary *is sitting on a tatty armchair.* **Mark** *is standing.*

Gary   Course, any day now it'll be virtual. That's what they reckon.

Mark   I suppose that's right.

Gary   I'm planning on that. Looking to invest. The Net and the Web and that. You ever done that?

Mark   No. Never.

Gary   Couple of years' time and we'll not even meet. We'll be like holograph things. We could look like whatever we wanted. And then we wouldn't want to meet 'cos we might not look like our holographs. You know what I mean? I think a lot about that kind of stuff me.
See, I called you back. Don't do that for everyone.

Mark   Thank you.

Gary   Why d'ya pick me?

Mark   I liked your voice.

Gary   There must have been something special.

Mark   I just thought you had a nice voice.

Gary   How old did you think I was – on the lines?

Mark   I didn't think about it.

Gary   How old do you want me to be?

Mark   It doesn't matter.

Gary   Everybody's got an age they want you to be.

Mark   I'd like you to be yourself.

Gary   That's a new one.

Mark   I'd like to keep things straightforward.

Gary   You're in charge. Make yerself at home.
D'you want porn? I mean, it's mostly women and that but
it's something.
(*Indicating porn.*) She looks rough, doesn't she? Would you
shag her?

Mark   No. Let's leave the porn.

Gary   Or we could do some like . . . stuff, y'know.

He pulls out a packet of cocaine.

Share it with you.

Mark   No. Thank you.

Gary   It's thrown in. There's no / extra cost.

Mark   I don't want any.

Gary   It's quality. He don't give me rubbish.

Mark   Put it away.

Gary   I int gonna poison ya.

Mark   Put the fucking stuff away.

Gary   Alright, alright. Don't get knocky.

Pause.

Mark   I'm going to have to go.

Gary   You only just got here.

Mark   I can't be around people who use.

Gary   Alright. Look. I'm putting it away.

He puts the packet in his trouser pocket.

See? All gone.
You stopping?

Mark   I'm sorry. I'm really sorry but I suppose I was
threatened by your actions. And my fear led me to an . . .
outburst. Which I now regret. It's just very important to me.
And I'd like you to acknowledge that.

Gary   You God Squad?

Mark   I'm sorry?

Gary   I had 'em before. We're at it and he kept going on
about Lamb of Jesus. Hit me. I give as good as I took.

Mark   No. I'm not God Squad.

Gary   Just got a thing about druggies?

Mark   I have a history of substance abuse.

Gary   You're a druggie?

Mark   I'm a recovering substance abuser.

Gary   You're not a druggie?

Mark   I used to be a druggie.

Gary   Got you. So what you into?

Mark   You mean . . .

Gary   Sexwise.

Mark   Sexwise, I'd say I'm into the usual things.

Gary   So, you're looking for regular?

Mark   Pretty regular. The important thing for me right
now, for my needs, is that this doesn't actually mean
anything, you know?
Which is why I wanted something that was a transaction.

Because I thought if I pay then it won't mean anything. Do you think that's right – in your experience?

Gary   Reckon.

Mark   Because this is a very important day for me. I'm sorry, I'm making you listen.

Gary   Everyone wants you to listen.

Mark   Right. Well. Today you see is my first day of a new life. I've been away to get better, well to acknowledge my needs anyway, and now I'm starting again and I suppose I wanted to experiment with you in terms of an interaction that was sexual but not personal, or at least not needy, OK?

A distant sound of coins clattering.

Gary   Downstairs. The arcade. Somebody's just had a win. You gotta know which ones to play otherwise all you get is tokens. I've a lucky streak me. Good sound, int it? Chinkchinkchinkchinkchink.

Mark   I suppose what I'd like, what I'd really like is to lick your arse.

Gary   That all?

Mark   Yes. That's all.

Gary   Right. We can settle up now.

Mark   How much do you want?

Gary   Hundred.

Mark   A hundred pounds? No, I'm sorry.

Gary   Alright. If it's just licking, fifty.

Mark   Look, I can give you twenty.

Gary   Twenty. What d'you expect for twenty?

Mark   It's all I've got.
I've got to keep ten for the taxi.

Gary   You're taking the piss, int ya?

Mark   Look, I'll walk. Thirty. It's all I've got.

Gary   I should kick you out, you know that? I shouldn't be wasting my time with losers like you. Look at you. Druggie with thirty quid. I'm in demand me. I don't have to be doing this.
There's a bloke, right, rich bloke, big house. Wants me to live with him.
So tell me: why should I let you lick my arse?

Mark   Why don't you think of him? You could lie there and think of him.
Just a few minutes, OK? Thirty quid.
Just get my tongue up, wiggle it about and you can think of him.
This isn't a personal thing. It's a transaction, OK?

Gary *pulls down his trousers and underpants.* **Mark** *starts to lick* **Gary***'s arse.*

Gary   He's a big bloke. Cruel like but really really he's kind. Phones me on the lines and says: 'I really like the sound of you. I want to look after you.'

Clatter of coins.

Listen to that. They're all winning tonight.
So I'll probably move in. Yeah, probably do it tomorrow.

Mark *pulls away. There's blood around his mouth.*

Mark   There's blood.

Pause.

You're bleeding.

Gary   Didn't think that happened any more.
Thought I'd healed, OK? That's not supposed to happen.
I'm not infected, OK?
Punter gave me a bottle somewhere. Rinse it out.

Mark *goes to take the money.*

Gary   You can't take that.
Lick me arse you said. Licked me arse didn't ya?

Mark   I'll leave you ten.

Gary   Rinse your mouth out.
We agreed thirty.

Mark   Twenty. I need ten for the taxi.

Gary   Thirty – look, I need the money – please – I owe
him downstairs – can't live on tokens – give me the thirty.
You promised.

Mark   Have the thirty.

Mark *gives* **Gary** *the thirty pounds.*

Gary   Stay. Rinse it out. You'll feel better. It's
champagne.

Gary *exits.* **Mark** *sits.*

Scene Five

Pub.

Robbie *hands* **Lulu** *a drink.*

Robbie   After ten minutes I thought I'd got the wrong
name. Checked the name. And then I thought: maybe it's
the right name but the wrong pub. Because there could be
two pubs with the same name. But probably not on the
same street. So I checked. And there wasn't. The same
name on this street. But then I thought there could be other
streets with the same street name. So I looked it up,
borrowed the book from this bloke and looked it – listen.
Did you know? There's blood.

Lulu   On me?

Robbie   On you. You've got blood on you face.

Lulu   I thought so. Get it off.

Robbie   Why's that then?

Lulu   Please I want it off.

Robbie   Is that your blood?

Lulu (*pawing at her face*)   Where is it?

Robbie (*indicates forehead*)   Just – yeah – that's it.

Lulu   Is it all gone? Everything?

Robbie   Yes. It's all gone.
Was that your blood?

Lulu   No. It must have splashed me.

Robbie   Who's blood is it?

Lulu   Why does it have to be like this?

Robbie   I knew something was up.

Lulu   I mean, what kind of planet is this when you can't
even buy a bar of chocolate?

Robbie   I think that's why I worried so much.

Lulu   And afterwards of course you feel so guilty. Like you
could have done something.

Robbie   They attacked you?

Lulu   Not me. The Seven-Eleven.
Walking past and I think: I'd like a bar of chocolate. So I go
in but I can't decide which one. There's so much choice.
Too much. Which I think they do deliberately. I'm only
partly aware – and really why should I be any more aware?
– that an argument is forming at the counter. A bloke.
Dirty, pissy sort of –

Robbie   Wino?

Lulu   Probably. Wino sort of bloke is having a go at this
girl, young –

Robbie   Student?

Lulu   Yes. Student girl behind the counter. Wino is raising his voice to student.

There's a couple of us in there. Me – chocolate. Somebody else – TV guides. (Because now of course they've made the choice on TV guides so fucking difficult as well.)

And wino's shouting: You've given me twenty. I asked for a packet of ten and you've given me twenty.

And I didn't see anything. Like the blade or anything. But I suppose he must have hit her artery. Because there was blood everywhere.

Robbie   Shit.

Lulu   And he's stabbing away and me and TV guide we both just walked out of there and carried on walking.

And I can't help thinking: why did we do that?

Robbie   Look. It's done now.

Lulu   I could have stayed.

Am I clean?

Robbie   All gone.

Lulu   I could have intervened. Stopped him.

It's all off?

Robbie   Yes.

Lulu   It's like it's not really happening there – the same time, the same place as you. You're here. And it's there.

And you just watch.

I'm going back.

Robbie   What for?

Lulu   Who called an ambulance? She could be lying there.

Robbie   No. There must have been someone.

Lulu   Or I could give a description.

Robbie   Did you see his face?

Lulu   No. No, I didn't.

Robbie He's a wino. How they going to find a wino out there?

Lulu I don't know.

Robbie Look, they'll have a video. There's always like a security camera. They'll have his face.

Lulu And I've still got. You see I took.

She produces the chocolate bar from her pocket.

I took the bar of chocolate. She's being attacked and I picked this up and just for a moment I thought: I can take this and there's nobody to stop me. Why did I do that? What am I?

Pause.

Robbie They must be used to it. Work nights in a shop like that, what do they expect?
You go home.

Lulu I can't.

Robbie You've had a shock. You need to rest.

Lulu We've got to do this.

Robbie I know.

Lulu We've got to do it tonight.

Robbie You're in no fit state. You've gotta sleep.

Lulu I don't want to sleep. I want to get on with this.

Robbie I'll do it.

Lulu We've got to do it together.

Robbie Think I can't manage? I can cope.

Lulu Of course you can.

Robbie I want to do it.

Lulu Out there on your own?

Robbie   I'm educated. I've read the books. I've got the bits of paper. It's only selling. I can sell. Go home. Go to bed.

Lulu   You're right. I am tired.

Robbie   Then sleep.

Lulu   They'll have me on the video. With the chocolate.

Robbie   They'll be after him. Not you.

Lulu   Suppose.
It's all here.

Lulu *give* **Robbie** *a bum-bag.*

Robbie   Right then.

Lulu   Look there's just one rule, OK? That's what they reckon. If you're dealing. There's just rule number one. Which is: He who sells shall not use.

Robbie   Yeah. Makes sense, doesn't it?

Lulu   Right. So just don't . . .

Robbie   Course not. Rule number one. I'm a big boy.

Lulu (*hands* **Robbie** *flyer*)   Show them this on the door.

Robbie   Still love you.

Lulu   Haven't said that for a long time. Wish we could go back to before. Just you and me.
Do you think I look great?

Robbie   In the right light. And a fair wind.

Lulu   And a couple of E?

Robbie   . . . I better go.

Exit **Robbie**.

Lulu *looks at the chocolate bar for a beat. Then eats it very quickly.*

Scene Six

Bedsit.

Gary *hands* **Mark** *the bottle of champagne.*

Gary   Horrible int it? Little kid with his arse bleeding.

Mark   Sorry. I need to go.

Gary   Arse like a sore.

Mark   It's not that.

Gary   Thought I'd healed.

Mark   Yes, yes. Sure.

Gary   This bloke, my mum's bloke . . .

Mark   No. Don't, please.

Gary   I tried to fight him off, but I think he gets off on that.

Mark   Please, if you . . .

Gary   Whatever, you lie back, you fight, he still . . .
I started to bleed.

Mark   No.

Gary   He comes into my room after *News at Ten* . . . every night after *News at Ten* and it's, son. Come here, son. I fucking hate that, 'cos I'm not his son.

Mark   Sure, sure. I understand.

Gary   But I thought . . . now . . . I . . . got . . . away.

Mark   FUCKING SHUT UP OK? KEEP YOUR FUCKING MOUTH SHUT.

Gary   Sound like him.

Mark   Listen. I want you to understand because. I have this personality you see? Part of me that gets addicted. I have a tendency to define myself purely in terms of my

relationship to others. I have no definition of myself you see.
So I attach myself to others as a means of avoidance, of
avoiding knowing the self. Which is actually potentially very
destructive. For me – destructive for me. I don't know if
you're following this but you see if I don't stop myself I
repeat the patterns. Get attached to people to these
emotions then I'm back to where I started. Which is why,
though it may seem uncaring, I'm going to have to go.
You're gonna be OK?
I'm sorry it's just –

Gary *cries.*

Mark   Hey. Hey. Hey.

He makes a decision. He takes **Gary** *in his arms.*

Come on. No. Come on. Please. It's OK.
Everything will be OK.
You don't have to say anything.

Gary   I want a dad. I want to be watched. All the time,
someone watching me. Do you understand?

Mark   I think so.

Gary   Does everyone feel like that?

Mark   Well . . . no.

Gary   What do you want?

Mark   I don't know yet.

Gary   You must want something. Everybody's got
something.

Mark   I used to know what I felt. I traded. I made money.
Tic Tac. And when I made money I was happy, when I lost
money I was unhappy. Then things got complicated. But for
so many years everything I've felt has been . . . chemically
induced. I mean, everything you feel you wonder . . . maybe
it's just the . . .

Gary   The smack.

Mark   Yes. The smack, coffee, you know, or the fags.

Gary   The microwaves.

Mark   The cathode rays.

Gary   The madcow. Moooooo.

Mark   Right. I mean, are there any feelings left, you know?

The coins clatter.

I want to find out, want to know if there are any feelings left.

Gary (*offering two Pot Noodles*)   Beef or Nice and Spicy?

Scene Seven

Accident and Emergency waiting room.

Robbie *sits bruised and bleeding.* **Lulu** *is holding a bottle of TCP.*

Lulu   I asked the Sister. She said I could. It'll sting a bit. But with blood. It might get infected. Like gangrene.

Lulu *applies the TCP to* **Robbie**'s *face.*

Lulu   Keep still. Don't want to end up with like – one eye mmm?
Look good actually.

Robbie   Yeah.

Lulu   Yes, suits you. Makes you look – well . . . tough.

Robbie   Good.

Lulu   I could go for you. Some people a bruise, a wound, doesn't suit them.

Robbie   No.

Lulu   But you – it fits. It belongs.

Lulu *slips her hand into* **Robbie***'s trousers and starts to play with his genitals.*

Lulu   Is that good?

Robbie   Yeah.

Lulu   That's it. Come on. That's it.
Tell me about them.

Robbie   Who?

Lulu   The men. Attackers.

Robbie   Them.

Lulu   The attackers. Muggers

Robbie   Well.

Lulu   Sort of describe what they did. Like a story.

Robbie   No.

Lulu   I want to know.

Robbie   It's nothing.

Lulu   I don't want to just imagine.

Robbie   I wasn't like that.

Lulu   Come on then.

Robbie   Look.

Lulu   What was it like?

Pause.

Robbie   There was only one.

Lulu   Didn't you say gang?

Robbie   No.
Just this one bloke.

Lulu   A knife?

Robbie   No.

Lulu   Oh.
So. He pinned you down?

Robbie   No.

Lulu   Got the money.

Robbie   I didn't – there wasn't any money alright? I never took any money.

Lulu   You never / sold?

Robbie   No.

Lulu   So before you even got there this man. With his knife –

Robbie   / There wasn't a knife.

Lulu   Attacks and gets the E.

Robbie   No. I got there. I was there with the E.

Lulu   So?

Robbie   So.

Pause.

Lulu   You've lost it. (*His erection.*)

Robbie   Yeah.

Lulu   Gone limp on me.

Robbie   Yeah.

Lulu   Why's that then?

Pause.

Robbie   I was there. I was all ready. I was ready to deal.

Lulu   Right.

Robbie   There's a few other dealers. Stood around the dance floor. I take up my position. I'm ready.
And this bloke comes up to me. Really, really nice-looking.

And he says: 'You selling?' Yeah, I say. Fifteen quid a go.
And the way he looks at me I know he fancies me, you
know?
And he reaches in his pocket and – oh shit. So stupid.

Lulu It was the knife yes?

Robbie There wasn't a knife.

Lulu Gun?

Robbie He. Look. He reaches in his pocket and says:
'Shit I left my money in my other jeans. Oh shit, now how
am I gonna have a good time, now how am I gonna enjoy
myself?'

Lulu Right. Yes.
Go on.

Robbie And he looked so . . . I felt sorry for him, alright?
But then he says: 'How about this? How about you give me
the E? Give me the E now then later, at the end, you can
come back to mine and we can get the money from my
jeans.'

Lulu Right so he was luring you. Luring you back to his /
place.

Robbie No.

Lulu Get you back to his so that he could pull the gun /
or whatever.

Robbie No.

Lulu And get the Es off you.

Robbie No, it didn't happen. That's not it.

Lulu No?

Robbie No.
So I said yes. It's a deal. And I gave him the E and he takes
it and I watch him and he's dancing and he's sweating and

smiling and he looks – well – beautiful and just really really happy.

Lulu   How many?

Robbie   What?

Lulu   You broke the first rule – yes? Yes?

Robbie   Yes.

Lulu   How many?

Robbie   I was out there on my own.

Lulu   How many?

Robbie   Three. Maybe four.

Lulu   Shit. I told you. Rule number one.

Robbie   I know.
But then, a few minutes later. A bloke. Even better, yes, even better looking than the last bloke. And he says: 'Look, you gave my mate some E and I was wondering, I get paid at the end of the week and if I give you my phone number will you give me a couple of E?'

Lulu   You didn't?

Robbie   Yes.

Lulu   Fuck.

Robbie   And I felt good, I felt amazing, from just giving, you see?

Lulu   No, no I don't.

Robbie   But imagine. Imagine you're there, imagine how it feels.

Lulu   No.

Robbie   And then – it sort of rolled. It flew.

Lulu   You prick. Three hundred.

Robbie   Until there's these guys, they're asking and I'm giving and everyone's dancing and smiling.

Lulu   Three hundred E. / Silly prick.

Robbie   Listen, listen to me. This is what I felt.

Lulu   I don't want to know. / You gave away three hundred.

Robbie   It's important.

Lulu   No. Stupid. Fucking. / Cunt.

Robbie   Just listen for a moment, OK?
Listen, this is the important bit. If you'd felt . . . I felt.
I was looking down on this planet. Spaceman over this earth. And I see this kid in Rwanda, crying, but he doesn't know why. And this granny in Kiev, selling everything she's ever owned. And this president in Bogota or . . . South America. And I see the suffering. And the wars. And the grab, grab, grab.
And I think: Fuck Money. Fuck it. This selling. This buying. This system. Fuck the bitching world and let's be . . . beautiful. Beautiful. And happy. You see?
You see?
But now you see, but then I've only got two left and this bloke comes up and says: 'You the bloke giving out the E?' I give him the two but he says 'What two? Two. Two's not going to do shit for me. You gotta have more.' And he starts to hit, he starts to punch me.

Lulu   Fucking fucker arsehole. Fuck.
Pillowbiter. (*Hit.*) Shitstabber. (*Hit.*)
Boys grow up you know and stop playing with each other's willies. Men and women make the future. There are people out there who need me. Normal people who have kind tidy sex and when they want it. And boys? Boys just fuck each other.
The suffering is going to be handed out. And I shouldn't be part of that. But it'll be both of us. And that's not justice. Is it?

You look like shit now. Look like you might get (*Throws the bottle of TCP into* **Robbie**'s *eyes.*) gangrene.

Exit **Lulu**.

Robbie   Nurse. Nurse.

Scene Eight

Bedsit.

Mark *and* **Gary**.

Gary   I knew it wasn't right. I went to the council.
And I said to her, look, it's simple: he's fucking me.
Once, twice, three times a week he comes into my room.
He's a big man. He holds me down and he fucks me. How long? she says. About two years, I say. I say he moved in then six months later it starts. I told her and she says 'Does he use a condom?'

Mark   Yeah?

Gary   Yeah. I mean 'Does he use a condom?'
When it's like that he's not gonna use a condom, is he? Just spit. All he used is a bit of spit.

Mark   On his – ?

Gary   Spit on his dick.

Mark   Of course.

Gary   And then she / says –

Mark   / And you –

Gary   The next thing / she says –

Mark   Does he / spit –

Gary   I told her that and / she says –

Mark   Does he spit up you?

Gary   Listen. I tell her he's fucking me – without a condom – and she says to me – you know what she says?

Mark   No. No, I don't.

Gary   I think I've got a leaflet. Would you like to give him a leaflet?

Mark   Fuck.

Gary   Yeah. Give him a leaflet.

Mark   Well –

Gary   No, I don't want a leaflet. I mean, what good is a fucking leaflet? He can't even read a fucking leaflet, you know.

Mark   Yes.

Gary   And there's this look – like . . . panic in her eyes and she says: What do you want me to do?

Mark   Right.

Gary   Tell me what you want me to do.

Mark   And you said.

Gary   Well, I don't know. Inject him with something, put him away, cut something off. Do something. And I'm – I've got this anger, right? This great big fucking anger – here in front of my eyes. I mean, I fucking hate her now, right?

Mark   So did you / attack?

Gary   I go: Fuck. Fuck.

Mark   Maybe a knife or something?

Gary   So. In this little box, little white box room . . .

Mark   You attacked / her?

Gary   I stand on the table and I shout:
It's not difficult this is it? It's easy this. He's my stepdad.
Listen, he's my stepdad and he's fucking me.

And I walk away and I get on the coach and I come down here and I'm never going back. Gonna find something else. Because there's this bloke. Looking out for me. He'll come and collect me. Take me to this big house/

Mark Look, this person that you're looking for . . .

Gary Yeah?

Mark Well it's not me.

Gary Of course not.

Mark No.

Gary Fuck, you didn't think . . . ? No. It's not meant to be you. You and me we're looking for different things, right?

Mark Right.

Gary Mates?

Mark Mates.

Gary So – mate – do you wanna stay?

Mark I don't know.

Gary Stay if you like. Room on the floor. Someone waiting up for you?

Mark Not exactly.

Gary You stay long as you want.

Mark Thank you.

Gary Stay around and you can keep yourself busy. Give us a hand. Getting the messages, cleaning up. Chucking out the mental ones.
Tell you what, you hang around long enough we can . . .

He pulls out a holdall from behind the chair.
He unzips the bag. It is full of fifty-pence pieces. He catches up handfuls and lets them cascade through his fingers.

See? I'm a winner me. Every time. And I don't let them give me tokens.
I can pay for what I want.
Stick around, you and me could go shopping yeah?

Mark   I don't know.

Gary   It's only shopping.

Mark   Alright then. Yeah. Let's go shopping.

*They both listen to the coins as they run through **Gary***'s fingers.*

Scene Nine

Flat.

Brian, **Lulu** *and* **Robbie**. **Brian** *inserts a video.*

Brian   Watch. I want you to see this.

*They watch a video of a schoolboy playing a cello. They sit for some time in silence. **Brian** starts to weep.*

Sorry. Sorry.

Lulu   Would you like a – something to wipe?

Brian   Silly. Me a grown man.

Lulu   Maybe a handkerchief?

Brian   No. No.

He pulls himself together. They sit and watch again for some time, but eventually he starts to weep again.

Oh God. I'm so – I'm really sorry.

Lulu   No, no.

Brian   It's just the beauty, you see? The beauty of it.

Lulu   Of course.

Brian   Like a memory, you know, memory of what we've lost.

Pause.

Lulu   Are you sure you don't want – ?

Brian   Well –

Lulu   It's no problem.

Brian   Well then.

Lulu (*to* **Robbie**)   Could you – ?

Robbie   No problem.

Robbie *exists. They continue to watch the video.* **Robbie** *enters again with a toilet roll, takes it over to* **Brian**.

Brian   What's this?

Robbie   It's for your – you know to wipe your -

Brian   I asked you what it is.

Robbie   Well.

Brian   So tell me what it is. What is in your hand?

Robbie   Well –

Lulu   Darling.

Brian   Yes?

Robbie   Toilet paper.

Brian   Toilet paper exactly. Toilet paper. Which belongs in the –

Robbie   Toilet.

Brian   Exactly.

Lulu   Darling, I didn't mean . . . that.

Brian   And we use it to – ?

Robbie   Well, wipe your arse.

Brian   Exactly. Wipe your arse. While I – what is this? (*Wipes eye.*)

Lulu   I didn't mean toilet paper.

Robbie   It's a – like a tear.

Brian   It is a tear. Little drop of pure emotion. Which requires a – ?

Robbie   Well, a hanky.

Brian   Handkerchief.

Robbie   Handkerchief.

Lulu   Of course, I meant a handkerchief.

Brian   This is disrupting you know that?

Lulu   Sorry.

Brian   This isn't – we're not in a supermarket or, or a disco. Music like this, you listen.

Lulu   Yes.

Again they all settle down to watch the video. After a while, **Brian** *starts to cry, but even more so this time.*

Brian   Oh God. Oh God. God.

Lulu   He's very good.

Brian   You feel it like – like something you knew. Something so beautiful that you've lost but you'd forgotten that you've lost it. Then you hear this.

Lulu   Play like that when he's how . . . how old?

Brian   Hear this and knew what you've . . . l-l-l-ooost.

Brian *starts to sob heavily.*

Lulu   Look, I think I've got one.

Robbie   A handkerchief?

Lulu   Yes. A handkerchief. In the bedroom.

Robbie   Shall I fetch it?

Lulu   Well – yes. Yes, I think you should.

Exit **Robbie**.

Brian   Because once it was paradise, you see? And you could hear it – heaven singing in your eyes. But we sinned, and God took it away, took away music until we forgot we even heard it but sometimes you get a sort of glimpse – music or a poem – and it reminds you of what it was like before all the sin.

Enter **Robbie**, *offers handkerchief to* **Brian**.

Brian   Is it clean?

Robbie   Yes.

Brian   Again – is it clean?

Robbie   Yes.

Brian   Again – is it clear?

Robbie   Yes.

Brian   Look me in the eyes. Straight in the eyes. Yes?

Robbie (*does so*)   Yes.

Brian   And again – is it clean?

Robbie   No.

Brian   Then why did you offer it to me?

Robbie   Well –

Brian   Dirty handkerchief. Offer a dirty handkerchief.

Lulu   Darling –

Brian   Handkerchief for your nose.

Brian *punches* **Robbie**. *He slumps to the floor.*

Robbie   I'm – sorry.

Lulu   Take it away.

Robbie   Yes. Sorry.

Robbie *crawls out as they settle down in front of the video.*

Brian   His teacher says – and it's a religious school, very religious school – his teacher says 'It's a gift from God.' And I think that's right. Think that must be right because it can't be from us. Doesn't come from me and his mother. I mean, where does it come from if it's not from God, eh? Kid like that, nice kid – his father's son – but nothing special, picks up a bit of wood and string and – well – grown men cry.

Lulu   You must be very proud.

Robbie *enters.* **Brian** *removes a pristine handkerchief from his top pocket and carefully wipes his eyes.*

Brian (*to* **Robbie**)   See. You don't wipe your eyes with something that's been up your nose, alright?

Robbie   Yes. Sorry.

They continue to watch the video.

Brian   Think of the life he's gonna have, eh? Think of that.

Pause.

Because he doesn't know it now of course. But when he's older, when he knows about sin, about all this, then he's gonna thank God he's got this, isn't he? This little bit of purity.

Lulu   It is amazing, isn't it?

Robbie   Yeah. Yeah. Really – amazing.

Lulu   That it just looks so effortless.

Brian   But there is effort.

Lulu   Of course.

Brian   Behind it all is effort.

Lulu   Have to practise all the time, don't they?

Brian   His effort – yes.

Lulu   For like – hours a day.

Brian   His efforts – of course – but also my efforts.

Lulu   Of course.

Brian   Because, at the end of the day, at the final reckoning, behind beauty, behind God, behind paradise, peel them away and what is there? (*To* **Robbie**.) Son, I'm asking you.

Robbie   Well –

Brian   Come on, son.

Robbie   Well –

Brian   Answer the question.

Robbie   Well – a father.

Brian   Sorry?

Robbie   You've can't have them without a sort of a dad.

Brian   No. No. Think again. Try again.

Robbie   Well I –

Brian   Think.

Robbie   No.

Brian   No, no. That's not good enough – no. Behind beauty, behind God, behind paradise –

Lulu   Darling . . . ?

Robbie   Money.

Brian   Yes. Good. Excellent. Money. Takes a few knocks, doesn't it, son?
Yeah.

But we get it knocked into us don't we, eh? Learn the rules.
Money. There's boarding fees and the uniforms, the gear,
the music, skiing.
Which is why I run such a tight ship you see? Which is why
I have to keep the cash flow flowing you see? Which is why I
can't let people FUCK. ME. AROUND. You understand?

Lulu   Of course.

Brian   Which is why, right now, I feel sad and sort of
angry. Yes?

Lulu   Yes.

Brian   I don't like mistakes. I don't like my mistakes. And
now you tell me I've made a mistake. And so I hate myself.
Inside. My soul.
We have a problem. Three thousand pounds of a problem.
But what is the solution?

They sit for a moment and contemplate this. Finally, **Brian** *gets up,
ejects the video, puts it back into its case.*

This could be a stalemate. Unless one of us concedes. But
would you concede? Could you concede anything?

Lulu   No.

Brian   So what you're saying is – you're asking me to
concede.

Lulu   Yes.

Brian   You think I should concede?

Long pause.

Seven days. To make the money.

Lulu   Thank you.

Brian   You understand? Son?

Robbie   Yes. Seven Days. Yes.

Pause. **Brian** *produces a second video.*

Brian   I'd like you to have a look at this. Camera's a bit shaky. Some people will tell you it's about 'production values'. But really . . . 'production values'? They're nothing without a good subject.

This one was recorded a couple of months ago. 11.53am. On a Wednesday.

He inserts the video, presses play: a Black and Decker being switched on.

You can't see the face, of course, but the hand belongs to one of my group.

Now a shot of a man with insulation tape over his mouth.

The man with the tape over his mouth is someone who failed his test.

The drill is moving towards the man's face.

There is so much fear, so much wanting. But we're all searching.
Searching aren't we?

Exit **Brian**.

Lulu *and* **Robbie** *watch as the video continues.*

Scene Ten

Flat. **Robbie** *is on the phone.*

Robbie   Come on. Take it.
This is . . . it's a golden opportunity. We could change the course of history.

A mobile phone starts to ring. **Lulu** *enters.*

That's what I say. Standing in the Garden and it's: All of humanity, the course of history. / Look, I'm offering it to you. Because we are the first, we are the only ones. And I want you to take it.

Lulu (*on mobile*)   / Hello. Hello, Terry.
No. You call as often as you like.
Oh good. Yes, that's a good idea. A cord that reaches the
bed.
Now, if you give me the number again. Yes.
And the expiry date. (*A second mobile rings.*) Yes.
Now I'm taking you into another.
Yes. I'm taking you into the bedroom.

Exit **Lulu**.

Robbie   Here in my hand. Skin. Core. Red. Red skin.
And there's juice.
And you see the juice and you want to bite.
Bite. Yes. Your tongue. The apple. Good. The forbidden
fruit.

(*Answers second mobile.*) Yes? For the . . . ? If you can . . . ?
She's just. Yes. Coming. On her way. Yes.

(*To phone.*) And it's like you've never seen before, you've
never looked at my body.

(*To second mobile.*) If you can wait, if you can hang on.
Because we're really very . . . sure, sure. A couple of
minutes.

(*To phone.*) My, my cock. It's hard. And what's there between
your . . . yes . . . because oh look you've got one too . . . that
you've never noticed . . . yes. Your own big cock.

(*To second mobile.*) Still there? Still holding? So, you're done.
Another time. Of course.

(*To phone.*) And you want me and I want you and it's man on
man and I'm Adam and you're Adam.

The second mobile starts to ring again.

And you want to take it right up the . . . yes . . . oh yes . . .
/ up against the Tree of Knowledge.

Enter **Lulu**, *still on first mobile.*

Lulu   / Smack. Smack. Smack.
Good. Good. Yes. Yes.

She puts down the first mobile and answers the second mobile.

Hello?
The name?
And the number.
Ah. Gallop. Yes.
Gallop apace you fiery-footed steeds towards Phoebus'
lodging! Such a waggoner as Phaeton would whip . . .
Yes . . .
Spread thy . . .
Good, that's right
Come, civil night. Come, gentle night. Come, loving black-
browed night. Come, Romeo.
Yes, nearly oh yes.
Oh I have bought the mansion of a love but have not
possessed it, and though I am sold not yet enjoyed.
Dirty fucking cunting fucker.
Yes. Yes. Good. Good. Bye then. Bye.

Robbie (*on phone*)   This is, I tell you this is Paradise. This is
Heaven on the Earth. And the spheres are sphering and the
firm . . .
Good good.
And now we're in the . . . ? Tower of . . . I see . . . the
Tower of Babel. All the tongues in the world. Splashinsky.
Mossambarish. Bam bam bam. Pashka pashka pashka.
Alright then. You're done? Good good. That's good. You
take care now. Yeah.

(*To* **Lulu**.)   Nine hundred pounds and seventy-eight pence.

Lulu   Why are there so many sad people in this world?

Robbie   We're making money.

Lulu   Yeah. Making money.

Robbie   We're gonna be all right.

Scene Eleven

Changing room at Harvey Nichols. **Mark** *is trying on an expensive designer suit.*

Gary (*off*)   How's it going?

Mark   Yeah. Good.

Gary   Do you want the other size?

Mark   No. This is great.

Gary   Alright then.

Mark   Have a look if you like.

Enter **Gary**. *He is transformed: top to toe designer gear and carrying bundles of expensive shopping bags.*

Gary   Oh yes.

Mark   Like it?

Gary   Oh yeah. It's you. Suits you. Do you want it?

Mark   I don't know.

Gary   If you like it, you have it.

Mark   I mean, it's not like I'm ever gonna wear it.

Gary   You don't know that. You're starting over.

Mark   I do like it.

Gary   Could be anything. New life, new gear. It makes sense. Go on.

Mark   You sure you can / afford . . . ?

Gary   Hey. None of that.

Mark   Alright then. Yes.

Gary   Good and now we'll . . .

He holds out a handful of credit cards as if they were playing cards.

Pick a card, any card.

Mark *picks a card. Reads the name on it.*

Mark   P. Harmsden.

Gary   You remember? Last night. Poppers. Kept on hitting himself.

Mark   Ah. P. Harmsden.

Gary   Right then. Get it off and then we're eating out. My treat.

Mark   Why don't you . . . wait outside?

Gary   I'm not bothered.

Mark   Have a look round. I'll only be a few minutes.

Gary   Too late now. I've seen it.

Mark   Seen the . . . ?

Gary   Seen the hard-on.

Mark   Ah yes. The hard-on.

Gary   Must be aching by now. Up all day.
Is it the shopping does that?
You gotta thing about shopping?
Or is it 'cos of me?

Mark   Yes. That's right. It's because of you.

Gary   Right.
What's going on in your head?
I mean, I can see what's going on in your pants but what's in there?
Tell me.

Mark   Nothing. Look. It's just a physical thing, you know?

Gary   So why don't you say what you want. Do you want to kiss me?

Mark   Yes.

Gary   Go on then.

Mark   Listen, if we do . . . anything, it's got to mean
nothing, you understand?

Gary   Course.

Mark   If I feel like it's starting to mean something then I'll
stop.

Gary   You can kiss me like a gentle kiss. Me mum, she's
got a nice kiss.

Mark *kisses* **Gary**.

Gary   How was that?

Mark   Yes. That was alright.

Gary   How old do you think I am?

Mark   I don't know.

Gary   When you met me – what did you think?

Mark   I don't . . . sort of sixteen, seventeen.

Gary   Right. Bit more?

Mark   Bit more.

He kisses **Gary** *again. This time it becomes more sexual. Eventually,*
Mark *pulls away.*

No. I don't want this.

Gary   I knew it. You've fallen for me.

Mark   Fuck. I really thought I'd broken this, you know?

Gary   Do you love me? Is that what it is? Love?

Mark   I don't know. How would you define that word?
There's a physical thing, yes. A sort of wanting which isn't
love is it? No, That's well, desire. But then, yes, there's an
attachment I suppose. There's also that. Which means I
want to be with you, Now, here, when you're with me I feel

like a person and if you're not with me I feel less like a person.

Gary   So is that love then?
Say what you mean.

Mark   Yes.
I love you.

Gary   See.

Mark   But what I'd like to do – now that I've said that which was probably very foolish – what I'd like to do is move forward from this point and try to develop a relationship that is mutual, in which there's a respect, a recognition of the other's needs.

Gary   I didn't feel anything.

Mark   No?

Gary   When you kissed me. Nothing.

Mark   I see.

Gary   Which means . . . gives me the power, doesn't it? So I'll tell you. You're not what I'm after. I don't want it like that.

Mark   But over a period of time . . .

Gary   No.

Mark   You see, if you've never actually been loved –

Gary   I'm not after love. I want to be owned. I want someone to look after me. And I want him to fuck me. Really fuck me. Not like that, not like him. And, yeah, it'll hurt. But a good hurt.

Mark   But if you had a choice.

Gary   Then I wouldn't choose you. I want to be taken away. Someone who understands me.

Mark   There's no one out there.

Gary   Think just because you don't feel that way no one else does? There's lots of people who understand. And someone's gonna do it.
I'm going now.

Mark   Stay please. Please I . . .

Mark *kisses* **Gary**, *who pushes him away.*

Gary   That's not true about me mum. I don't let her kiss me. She's a slag.
You go home now. You go back where you belong.

Mark   I want to stay with you.
Give me a day, OK? Another day.

Gary   Don't waste your time with me.

Mark   You can . . . look yes. Come home with me.

Gary   What for? I'm nothing.

Mark   Show you where I live, who I live with.

Gary   You're pathetic you.

Mark   Just one more day. Give it a day.

Gary   You gonna take me home and fuck me?
Alright then. One day. Take me home.

Mark   Suck my cock.

Gary   You taking me home?

Mark   Suck my cock now. Take you home later.

Gary   There's a security camera.

Mark   Doesn't matter.

Gary   All this for me? Fourteen.
You got it wrong. I'm fourteen.

Scene Twelve

Robbie *and* **Lulu** *looking at the phone.*

Robbie   Come on. Ring. Ring.
This shouldn't be happening.
Why is this happening?
I mean, we're close really. Nearly two thousand. Over two
thousand – that's good, isn't it? We're very, very close.
We've been working. We're making money. We're good at
it, aren't we? Isn't that right? You'd say that's right,
wouldn't you?

Lulu   That's right.

Robbie   So, it can't stop now. They've got to keep on
coming.
Ring you bastard ring.
Shit. I can't stand it.

Lulu   It's just quiet. A quiet time. That happens.

Robbie   Hasn't happened before.

Lulu   Sit down. Relax.

Robbie   I can't.

Lulu   It'll start again.

Robbie   There isn't time. We can't afford this.

Lulu   Just a moment's peace. Make the most of it.

Robbie   I want to live. I want to survive, don't you?

Lulu   I don't know.

Robbie   You want to die?

Lulu   No. I want to be free. I don't want to live like this.

Robbie   That's right. Another day yeah?

Lulu   Yes.

Robbie   One more day and we'll be free.

Lulu   Yes.

Robbie   If it keeps on ringing.

Ping of a microwave.

Lulu   Food's ready.

Robbie   Yeah.

Lulu   Eat something?

Robbie   Yes.

Exit **Lulu**.

Robbie   Come on. Come on. Please.

He picks up the phone and speaks into it.

Why aren't you ringing you . . .

He realises that the line is dead.
Checks the lead – finds it's been pulled out of the wall.
Check the mobiles. They've been switched off.

Sits.

Enter **Lulu** *with microwave meals, offers one to* **Robbie**.

Robbie   No thanks.

Lulu   Eat something.

Robbie   No thanks.

Lulu   Come on.

Robbie   I'm not hungry.

Lulu   Alright then.

Pause.

Have a bit.

Robbie   Don't want any.

Lulu   Might as well have a meal while it's quiet.

Robbie   You reckon?

Lulu   It'll all start again in a minute.

Robbie   They'll all be ringing?

Lulu   Of course.

Robbie   Don't think so. Do you?

Lulu   Course they will.

Robbie   No. I reckon they're not gonna ring. I reckon that tomorrow we're gonna die.

Lulu   Course not.

Robbie   Because I reckon that one of us wants to die.

Lulu   No.

Robbie   No?

Lulu   No.

Robbie   Then tell me why one of us disconnected the phones.

Lulu   For a few moments. I just wanted / a few minutes peace.

Robbie   And I want to live. That's what I want to do.

Lulu   I just wanted to eat a meal without . . . all that.

Robbie   There'll be time later.

Lulu   I can't stand it. In my head.

Robbie   And what about me?
We've got to do this together.

Robbie *moves to reconnect the phone.*

Lulu   No. Please. Not yet.

Robbie   We have to carry on.

Lulu   After we've eaten this. Ten, five minutes.

Robbie Come on.

Lulu There was this phone call. I had this call. Twenty minutes, half hour ago. Youngish. Quite well spoken really. And I did the . . . you know . . . where are you sitting? In the living-room. Right. And you're . . . ? Yes, yes, playing with his dick. Good. Fine. So far, auto-pilot. And then he says, I'm watching this video. Well, that's good. And then he starts to . . . he describes . . . because he got this video from his mate who copied it from his mate who copied it from dahdahdah. And I mean, he's wanking to this video of a woman, a student girl who's in the Seven-Eleven, working behind the counter. And there's a wino and . . . yeah.

Robbie Fuck.

Lulu Yeah. He was wanking to the video.
So if we can just. A few more minutes.

Robbie No. We're gonna carry on.

Lulu Eat something first.

Robbie There's no time.

Lulu Eat. Eat. Eat first. Few minutes.

Robbie I'm not eating.

Lulu What's wrong with the / . . . Look, if I'm eating . . . If I can . . .

Robbie I don't want the food, / it doesn't taste of anything . . .

Lulu And why? / What is so wrong that you can't eat it?

Robbie I'm not eating. / There isn't time.

Lulu Come on, you've got the world here. You've got all the tastes in the world. You've got an empire under cellophane. Look, China. India. Indonesia. In the past you'd have to invade, you'd have to occupy just to get one of these things and now, when they're sitting here in front of you, you're telling me you can't taste anything.

Lulu *holds* **Robbie** *back to prevent him reconnecting the phone.*

Robbie   Well, yes. Yes I am. / There's no taste. This stuff tastes of nothing.

Lulu   Eat it. Eat it. Eat it.

Robbie   This stuff?

Lulu   Now. Eat it now.

Robbie   No. This? This is shit. / This? I wouldn't feed a fuckng paraplegic with cancer this shit.

Lulu   Eat it. Eat it. Eat it. Eat it.

Lulu *pushes* **Robbie**'*s face into the food.*

Enter **Mark** *and* **Gary**.

Mark   Hello.

Robbie   Where have you been?
You went out to get chocolate. A week ago.
Chocolate or a cheeseburger from the shop.
So why have you brought him back?

Mark   Show him where I live.

Robbie   Been shopping? How did you pay for all that?

Mark   He paid.

Gary   Yeah. Paid for everything.

Mark   Who I lived with.

Robbie   And here we are. I'm Barney, this is Betty. Pebbles is playing outside somewhere. And you must be Wayne.

Gary   Wayne? I'm not Wayne. Who's Wayne?

Lulu   We're just eating. Sitting down for a meal. It's actually very difficult to share them actually because they're specifically designed as individual portions but I can get an extra plate. Plate. Knife. Whatever.

Mark   No no no. I don't think we're that hungry.

Robbie   We? We? Listen to that: we.

Mark   Well, I don't think we are.

Gary   Didn't come round to eat, did we?

Mark   No, no, we didn't, no.

Robbie   You on special offer?

Gary   You what?

Robbie   Cheaper than a Twix?

Gary   He don't need to pay me.

Robbie   Really? He will do. He's got this thing. Has to make it a transaction.

Gary   Not with me.

Lulu   It all got a bit messy.

Robbie   Paid Wayne, didn't you?

Mark   Gary, this is Lulu.

Lulu   Things got out of hand.

Gary   Some people you just give it away, don't you?

Lulu   Let's sit down, shall we? Let's all just sit.

They sit.

Well, look at this mess. If you don't watch yourself, you just revert, don't you? To the playground or canteen and suddenly it's all food fights and mess.
So let's be adults. Not much but I think I can still . . . a portion. Anyone?
Darling?

Mark   No.

Robbie   So – you're special?

Gary   He thinks so.

Robbie   He said that? He told you that?

Mark   Come on now. Leave him alone.

Gary   Yes. He said that.

Robbie   Tell me.

Mark (*to* **Robbie**)   Leave him alone.

Robbie   I want to know.

Lulu   Pudding is going to be quite a surprise I can tell you. / I'm really looking forward to pudding.

Robbie   Tell me what he said to you.

Gary   He said: I love you.

Mark   It wasn't those words.

Gary   Yeah, yeah. I love you. I'd be lost without you.

Mark   I never said those words.

Robbie (*to* **Gary**)   You're lying. Fucking lying.

Robbie *leaps on* **Gary** *and starts to strangle him.*

Gary   No. It's true. Please. 'S true. He loves me.

Mark   Leave him alone. Get off. Off.

Mark *attacks* **Robbie**, *who is attacking* **Gary**.
Lulu *tries to protect the ready meals, but most are crushed in the melee.*

Lulu   Stop it. Stop. Now.

Mark *succeeds in pulling* **Robbie** *off* **Gary**. *The fight subsides.*

Gary   Loony. You're a fucking headcase, you are.

Lulu   Come on leave it now leave it.

Gary   Fucking going for me.

Lulu   Ssssh . . . quiet . . . quiet.

Long pause.

Robbie   'I love you.'

Lulu   Forget it.

Robbie   That's what he said you said.

Mark   I never said – because – look – I don't.

Exit **Mark**.

Lulu   Mess. Look at this. Why is everything such a mess?

Lulu *scrapes up as much as she can on to the tray and exits.*
Robbie *and* **Gary** *regard each other in silence.*

Gary   He *does* love me. He did say that.

Robbie   Did he do this thing – ask you to lick his balls while he came?

Gary   Yeah. Have you . . . ?

Robbie   Too many times. I'm his boyfriend.

Gary   He doesn't do nothing for me, alright?

Robbie   No? Not your type?

Gary   He's too soft.

Pause.

Do you love him?

Robbie   Yes.

Pause.

Gary   It's all gentle with him. That's not what I'm after. Got to find this bloke. I know he's out there. Just got to find him.

Robbie   Someone who's not gentle?

Gary   Yeah, something strong. Firm, you know.

Robbie   Yes.

Gary You think he's cruel but really he's looking out for you. I'm going to be somewhere. I'll be dancing. Shopping. Whatever. And he'll fetch me. Take me away.

Robbie If he exists.

Gary You what?

Robbie If he really exists.

Gary You saying I'm lying?

Robbie I didn't say that.
I think . . . I think we all need stories, we make up stories so that we can get by.
And I think a long time ago there were big stories. Stories so big you could live your whole life in them. The Powerful Hands of the Gods and Fate. The Journey to Englightenment. The March of Socialism. But they all died or the world grew up or grew senile or forgot them, so now we're all making up our own stories. Little stories. It comes out in different ways. But we've each got one.

Gary Yes.

Robbie It's lonely. I understand. But you're not alone. I could help. I'm offering to help. Where you gonna start? Maybe I know what you're looking for.

Gary A helping hand. What do you wanna do that for?

Robbie For a fee.

Gary Yeah?

Robbie Yeah. Pay me and you'll get what you want. I've got instincts. I know about this other bloke.

Gary If I get what I want.

Robbie Cash. It's got to be cash.

Gary Course.

Robbie You've got the money?

Gary   Yeah. I've got the money.
So. What you gonna do? To help me.

Robbie   We're gonna play a game.

Scene Thirteen

The flat.

Mark, **Gary**, **Lulu** *and* **Robbie**.

Mark   Why are we playing this?

Robbie   Because he wants to.

Mark   It's a stupid game.

Robbie   Your friend. Isn't that right?

Gary   Right.

Mark   Why do you want to play this?

Gary   In my head, I see this picture, alright?

Lulu   Yes.

Gary   Well, like a picture but like a story, you know?

Robbie   Yes?

Gary   A sort of story of pictures.

Lulu   A film?

Gary   Yeah, story like a film.

Robbie   With you?

Gary   Yes.

Lulu   You're in the film?

Gary   Yes.

Robbie   You're the hero – ?

Gary   Well –

Lulu   You're the protag – you are the central character of the film?

Gary   Sort of. Yeah.

Robbie   Right.

Gary   So there's this story, film and I – there's these stairs.

Pause.

Robbie   What?

Gary   No. Look, I don't want to . . .

Lulu   You don't want to –

Gary   I thought I could but I can't, alright?
It's just saying it. Sorry.

Robbie   So – just wasting our time?

Gary   I'm sorry.

Robbie   We should have got the money first.

Lulu   You're not going through with this?

Gary   I don't know.

Robbie   He should have paid up front.

Mark   Paying for . . . ?

Robbie   Paying to play the game.

Lulu   So do you want to do this?

Pause.

Robbie   Pointless. Wasting our time. I mean, how old are you? What are you? Some kid wasting our time.

Gary   I'm not a kid.

Robbie   You don't know what you want.

Gary   I know what I want.

Lulu   So . . . ?

Gary   It's just . . . the words. It's describing it.

Mark   Alright. Come back to him.

Robbie   Now, as I'm the judge –

Mark   Do me. Ask me – truth or dare?

Robbie   That's not fair. That's not in the rules, is it?

Mark   But if he's not ready.

Robbie   Right. A forfeit. Something I'd like you to . . . something by way of punishment.

Mark   Just leave it, OK?

Gary   Shit, I don't want to.

Robbie (*to* **Lulu**)   What do you think would be a suitable punishment?

Mark (*to* **Gary**)   It's alright. It's alright.

Gary   Shit.

Gary*'s tears are close to hysteria.*

Mark   I'll do it. We can come back to you.
Now – ask me a question.

Robbie   No.

Mark   Come on – ask me a question.

Lulu   Alright.

Robbie   It's cheating.

Lulu   I know. My question is . . . My question is: who is the most famous person you've ever fucked?

Mark   The most famous person?

Lulu   The most famous person.

Mark   Well OK then OK.

Robbie   If you're gonna . . . it's got to be the truth.

Mark   Yeah, yeah.

Robbie   Or it doesn't count.

Mark   I know.

Lulu   Come on. The most famous person.

Robbie   No because last time –

Lulu   Come on.

Robbie   No because before.

Lulu   Let him say it.

Robbie   You made it up last time.

Mark   I know, I know.

Robbie   So what I'm saying is –

Mark   I know what you're saying.

Robbie   I'm saying it's got to be true.

Mark   Right.

Beat.

Robbie   Right.

Beat.

Lulu   Well then –

Mark   Well then. I'm in Tramps, OK? Tramps or Annabel's, OK?

Robbie   Which – ?

Mark   I can't remember.

Robbie   Look, you've got to –

Lulu   Go on.

Mark   Tramps or Annabel's or somewhere, OK?

Robbie   If you don't know where.

Mark   It doesn't matter where, OK?

Robbie   If it's true then –

Mark   The place, the name doesn't matter.

Lulu   No. It doesn't matter.

Robbie   I think you should know –

Mark   What the fuck does it matter where?

Lulu   Alright.

Mark   When what you said was who.

Lulu   Come on. Who? Who? Who?

Mark   Tramps or Annabel's or someplace. Someplace because the place is not of importance, OK? Because the place doesn't matter. So I'm at this somewhere place –

Robbie   When?

Mark   Jesus.

Lulu   It doesn't matter.

Robbie   I want to know when.

Lulu   Come on, you're there and –

Robbie   I want to know when?

Mark   Sometime. In the past.

Robbie   The last week past? The last year past? Your childhood past?

Lulu   The past past.

Mark   Well I don't –

Robbie   Come on –

Lulu   Why?

Robbie   Veracity. For the /

Mark   / alright then alright /

Robbie   / veracity of it.

Mark   '84. '85. About then. OK?

Robbie   OK.

Mark   So I'm in this place – which is maybe Tramps maybe not – and it's possibly 1985 –

Robbie   That's all I wanted to know.

Mark   I'm having a good time.

Robbie   Meaning?

Mark   Meaning a good time. Meaning a time that is good.

Robbie   Meaning you've taken –

Mark   Meaning I'm having a time that is good.

Robbie   Because you've taken –

Mark   Not necessarily.

Robbie   But you had?

Mark   I don't know.

Robbie   Come on. '84. '85. You must have been on something.

Mark   Well yes.

Robbie   Yes.

Mark   Probably yes.

Robbie   Because really when can you say you're not –

Mark   What? Go on, what?

Robbie   When can you say you're not on something?

Mark   Now.

Robbie   Yeah?

Lulu   Come on. Come on.

Robbie   You're sure? Sure that you're not –

Mark   Yes.

Lulu   Let's – the story.

Mark   I'm fucking clean, alright?

Lulu   Come on. '84. '85. Tramps. Annabel's.

Robbie   Yeah. Right.

Mark   I mean, what the fuck do I have to – ? I'm clean, OK?

Lulu   Please. I want to know who.

Mark   Alright. Just don't – alright. Tramps. '84. I'm having a good time.

Robbie   You're tripping?

Mark   No. And I need a piss, yes?

Lulu   In the toilet?

Mark   Yes, a piss in the toilet.

Lulu   This is a toilet story.

Mark   So, I'm taking my way to the toilet, right? And there's this woman, OK? This woman is like watching me.

Lulu   Who? Who? Who?

Mark   Of course, I should have known then. I should have known who she was.

Lulu   Who?

Mark   But I mean I am so –

Robbie   You're tripping.

Mark   No.

Robbie   You should have known who she was but you're tripping.

Mark   Look, I was not tripping.

Robbie   You didn't recognise this famous person because you were completely out of it.

Mark   OK, OK, I was completely out of it.

Lulu   And you're on your way to the toilet.

Mark   Out of it. All I know is that this woman's eyes are like: give me your veiny bang stick, OK?

Lulu   Way with words.

Mark   So I'm pissing. Urinals. I'm pissing in the urinals and in the mirror I see the door, OK? Well, OK. Pissing and the door opens. Door opens and it's her.

Lulu   So you're what – in the ladies?

Robbie   Urinals in the ladies?

Mark   Nope.

Robbie   So this is the –

Mark   Urinals in the gents.

Robbie   So she's –

Mark   She's there in the gents, OK? Standing in the gents watching me piss, OK? And now, we're in like bright – we're in fluorescent light I see.

Lulu   Who? Who? Who?

Mark   Not yet.

Robbie   Why not?

Mark   Because I'm out of it, OK. As you say, I'm on something. I should know who, but I don't recognise her, OK?

Lulu   So then bright light and you see . . . ?

Mark   See what she's wearing. A uniform. She is wearing a police uniform.

Lulu   Fuck. Who? Who? Who?

Robbie   A man's uniform or – ?

Mark   WPC. The Docs, the stockings, the jacket. The works. The hat. And she looks me in the eyes –

Gary   A woman?

Robbie   You're pissing?

Mark   Looks me in the eyes by way of the mirror, OK?

Robbie   OK, OK.

Gary   You did it with a woman?

Mark   She looks, she, she, she cruises me and then goes into one of the cubicles but looking at me all the time, you know? Goes into one of the cubicles and leaves the door ajar. I want to race right in there, you know? Get down to it but, like you do, I count to ten. Count to ten and then like coolly walk past. And as I walk past I take a cool glance to my left, cool look into the cubicle, cubicle with the door ajar and – wow.

Lulu   Wow?

Mark   Wow? The skirt is up around the waist. The skirt is up and the knickers are off or maybe she never had knickers – who knows? – but the skirt is up and she is like displaying this beautiful, come and get it snatch to die for, OK?

Gary   Said you didn't go for women.

Robbie   Facing / you?

Lulu   Who is it?

Mark   So I'm in there. I'm in and I kneel. I pay worship. My tongue is worshipping that pussy like it's God. And that's when she speaks. Speaks and I know who she is.

Lulu   Who?

Mark   She says 'Oh yah. Chocks away.'

Lulu No.

Robbie What?

Gary Is this a woman?

Lulu No – it can't be.

Robbie I told you.

Lulu That is fucking unbelievable.

Robbie Yes, yes it is.

Lulu What? Fergie?

Mark Yup. Fergie.

Lulu Fucking hell.

Mark I recognise the voice. Get a look at the face. It's her.

Robbie Come on –

Mark Fergie is like 'chocks away'. Fergie is right down to it. Fergie is ready to swallow anything, you know? I mean, any chocks there might have been have been chocked away. So a couple of minutes later, I'm there and Fergie is fellating. It's gobbledeygobble up against the cistern.

Robbie Nobody believes this. How can you believe this?

Mark Gobbledeygobble and the door, door to the cubicle starts to open.

Robbie This is ridiculous.

Mark I haven't locked the door, you see.

Robbie We said the truth. It had to be the truth.

Mark Rule number one. Always lock the door.

Robbie No one believes this.

Mark   Door opens and there's another woman. Yes. There's a second woman. Another policewoman like squeezes her way in.

Robbie   Shut up.

Mark   With blonde hair.

Robbie   SHUT UP. SHUT THE FUCK UP.

Pause.

Mark   What? What I thought you wanted to know . . .

Robbie   The truth.

Mark   Which is what . . .

Robbie   No.
(*To* **Lulu**.) Do you believe him?
(*To* **Gary**.) Do you?

Pause.

Rule number one. Never believe a junkie.
Because a junkie is a cunt. And when a junkie looks you in the eyes and says 'I love you' that's when you know he's gonna fill you full of shit.

Pause.

Gary   Why didn't you tell me you'd done it with a woman?

Robbie (*to* **Gary**)   Back to you.

Gary   Alright.

Robbie   It's your turn now.

Mark   You don't have to –

Gary   I want to.

Lulu   We'll help you.

Gary   Yeah?

Lulu   Help you find the words.

Robbie Alright then. Alright. Your story. Your film, yeah?

Gary Yeah.

Robbie I think I know what it is. I see. I understand.

Gary Yeah.

Robbie Yes. These pictures in your head.

So if I help – yes? If I can help you to describe the pictures then –

Gary Yes.

Robbie Alright. Alright. There's you yes and you're. I see you . . . there's music yes?

Gary Music. Yes.

Robbie Loud music. Dum dum dum. Like / techno.

Gary Techno music. Yes.

Robbie Techno music and you're moving like – you're dancing yes?

Gary Dancing.

Robbie Dancing on a dance floor. Dance floor in a club.

Gary Yes. Yes. A club.

Robbie And you're dancing with this bloke.

Gary No. Not like that. He's just there.

Robbie Dancing by yourself. But now . . .

Gary Watching.

Robbie Bloke who's watching you.

Gary I'm dancing.

Lulu He's watching.

Gary Yeah. Watching me.

Lulu And you smile.

Gary No. No smile.

Robbie But you know, you think: you don't have a choice.

Lulu No control.

Gary No control.

Robbie Because he's . . .

Lulu Because he's . . .

Gary Because he's gonna / take me away.

Robbie Have you. I'm going to have you.

Lulu He's going to have you.

Mark Come on, leave –

Robbie No.

Mark This is – it's getting heavy.

Gary No.

Robbie We're getting to the truth.

Gary I want to do it.

Lulu Now there's another – a fat bloke.

Gary Yes? A fat bloke?

Lulu Fat bloke who owns you.

Gary I didn't know about him.

Lulu Owns you but doesn't want you.
And the fat blokes says:
See that one dancing?

Robbie Yeah. Yeah. I see him.

Lulu Well, he's mine. I own him.

Mark Fuck's sake.

Lulu I own him but I don't want him.

Gary   Dunt want me.

Lulu   You know something.
He's trash and I hate him.

Robbie   Hate him.

Gary   Right. Hates me.

Robbie   And the fat bloke says –

Lulu   Well, you wanna buy him?

Gary   Yes.

Robbie   And / I say.

Gary   You say.

Robbie   How much?

Lulu   Piece of trash like that. Well, let's say twenty. He's yours for twenty.

Robbie   So you see the money.

Gary   I see money. See you pay him.

Robbie   You've seen the . . .

Gary   Transaction. I've seen the transaction.

Robbie   Transaction.

Gary   Yes and you've come to fetch me. You don't say anything. Just take me away.

Robbie   Good. Take you away.

Gary   Big car. Through the security gates and we're in the house.
And now dark. I can't see because . . . I'm wearing a, there's like a . . .

Lulu   A blindfold?

Gary   Blindfold. Yes . . . like a blindfold.

Lulu *produces a blindfold.*

Mark *pushes* **Lulu** *away and put his arms around* **Gary**.

Mark   Alright. Stop now. See? You can choose this instead. You must like that.
Just to be loved.

Gary   What are you doing?

Mark   Just holding you.

Gary   You've not even fucked me.

He pushes **Mark** *away.*

You're taking the piss, aren't you?

Mark   I'm just trying to show you. Because, I don't think that you have ever actually been loved and if the world has offered us no practical . . .

Gary   What are you?

Mark   I can take care of you.

Gary   You're nobody. You're not what I want.

Mark   If you can just get out of this trap.

Gary   I don't want you. Understand? You're nothing.

Mark   Wait. I just need to get this.

Mark *takes coke from* **Gary**'s *pocket and retreats.*

Lulu   Do you understand what we're going to do to you?

Gary   Yes.

Lulu   You understand and do you want us to do this?

Gary   Yes.

Lulu *puts the blindfold on* **Gary**.

Robbie   Blindfold you and –

Gary   Take me up the stairs.

Robbie   In my house?

Gary   In your house.

Lulu *and* **Robbie** *spin* **Gary** *around.*

Robbie   And you feel . . . you know this house. Know you've been here before.

Gary   Yeah. When have I been here before?

Lulu   And now. Now a bare room.
So – you're the new slave?

Robbie   Yes. Yes, old woman. This is the new slave.

Lulu   Beware. Beware. Do you now what the last slave died of?

Gary   No. There's no woman.

Robbie   Now.

Lulu   Ssssssh. He's coming. The master is coming.
Sssssshhh.

Gary   I know this house. I know who he is.

Robbie   Knob. Knob on the door turning.

Silence. **Gary** *stands very still.* **Robbie** *slowly approaches him from behind. Long pause –* **Robbie** *inches away from* **Gary**.

Gary   Go on.

Robbie   Yes?

Gary   Do it.

Robbie   It's what you want.

Gary   Yes.

Robbie *starts to undo* **Gary**'s *trousers.*

Robbie   Yes?

Gary   Yes.

Robbie *pulls down* **Gary**'s *trousers.*

He spits on his hand. Slowly he works the spit up **Gary**'s *arse.*

Robbie   Now?

Gary   Do it now.

Robbie   Now.

Robbie *unzips his fly. Works spit on to his penis. He penetrates* **Gary**. *He starts to fuck him.*

Silence. **Robbie** *continues to fuck* **Gary**.

Lulu   Is that good? Do you like that?

More silent fucking.

Robbie (*to* **Mark**)   Do you want him?

Mark   I . . .

Robbie   Do you know what he is? Trash. Trash and I hate him. Want him, you can have him.

Mark   Yes.

Robbie *pulls away.* **Mark** *goes through the same routine – spitting and penetrating* **Gary**. *He fucks him viciously.*

Mark   Fuck you. Fuck you.

Lulu   Does it hurt? Is it hurting you?

Gary   Are you him? Are you my dad?

Mark   No.

Gary   Yes. You're my dad.

Mark   I told you – no.

He hits **Gary**.
Then, he pulls away from **Gary**.

Gary   See. See. I know who you are. So finish it.

Mark   No.

He hits **Gary** *repeatedly.*

I'm. Not. Your. Dad.

Lulu   Leave him. Leave him now. Finished. It's over.

Gary   No. Don't stop now.

Robbie   No?

Robbie *gets into position to continue fucking* **Gary**.

Gary   Because – look – this bit. It doesn't end like this.
He's always got something. He gets me in the room,
blindfolds me. But he doesn't fuck me. Well not him, not his
dick. It's the knife. He fucks me – yeah – but with a knife.
So . . .

Pause.

Lulu   No.

Mark   Gotta have something.

Gary   In the kitchen. Or, or a screwdriver. Or something.

Lulu   No.

Gary   Got to be fucking something. That's how it ends.

Robbie *pulls off* **Gary**'s *blindfold*.

Robbie   No. I can't do that.

Gary   You're not gonna finish like this?

Robbie   I'm not gonna do that.

Lulu   You'll bleed.

Gary   Yeah.

Lulu   You could die.

Gary   No. I'll be OK. Promise.

Robbie   It'll kill you.

Gary   It's what I want.

Lulu   Go home now.

Gary   Just do it. Just fucking do it.
You're losers – you're fucking losers you know that?

Robbie   Yeah.

Gary   Listen, right. When someone's paying, someone wants something and they're paying, then you do it.
Nothing right. Nothing wrong. It's a deal. So then you do it.
I thought you were for real.
Pretending, isn't it? Just a story.

Robbie   Yes. It's just a story.

Mark (*to* **Robbie** *and* **Lulu**)   Please leave us now.

Lulu   We needed his money.

Mark   I know. If you leave us alone. I'll take care of this.
Yes?

Lulu   Come on, come on.

Exit **Robbie** *and* **Lulu**.

Gary   Are you gonna do it? I want you to do it. Come on.
You can do it.
Because he's not out there.
I've got this unhappiness. This big sadness swelling like it's gonna burst.
I'm sick and I'm never going to be well.

Mark   I know.

Gary   I want it over. And there's only one ending.

Mark   I understand.

Gary   He's got no face in the story. But I want to put a face to him. Your face.

Mark   Yes.

Gary   Do it. Do it and I'll say 'I love you'.

Mark   Alright. You're dancing and I take you away.

Scene Fourteen

The flat.

Brian *has the holdall of money.*

Brian   You know, life is hard. On this planet. Intractable. I can tell you this because I feel it. Yes, like you I have felt this. We work, we struggle. And we find ourselves asking: what is this for? Is there meaning? I know you've . . . I can see this question in your eyes. You ask yourself these questions. Right now – yes?

Robbie   Yes.

Brian   And you – what is there to guide me on my lonely journey?
Yes?

Lulu   Yes.

Brian   We need something. A guide. A talisman. A set of rules. A compass to steer us through this everlasting night. Our youth is spent searching for this guide until we . . . some give up. Some say there is nothing. There is chaos. We are born into chaos. But this is . . . no. This is too painful. This is too awful to contemplate. This we deny. Am I right?

Robbie   Yes.

Brian   Yes. I have a rung a bell. Good, good. Bells are rung.
Chaos or . . . order. Meaning. Something that gives us meaning.

Pause.

My dad once said to me. My dad said it to me and now I'm going to say it to you. One day my dad says to me: Son, what are the first few words in the Bible?

Robbie   In the beginning.

Brian   No.

Robbie   Yes. In the beginning.

Brian   I'm telling you no.

Robbie   That's what it says. In the beginning.

Brian   No, son. I'm telling you no. And you listen to me
when I'm telling you no, alright?

Robbie   Alright.

Brian   Tell me, son, says my dad, what are the first few
words in the Bible? I don't know, Dad, I say, what are the
first few words in the Bible? And he looks as me, he looks
me in the eye and he says: Son, the first few words in the
Bible are . . . get the money first. Get. The Money. First.

Pause.

It's not perfect, I don't deny it. We haven't reached
perfection. But it's the closest we've come to meaning,
Civilisation is money. Money is civilisation. And civilisation
– how did we get here? By war, by struggle, kill or be killed.
And money – it's the same thing, you understand?
The getting is cruel, is hard, but the having is civilisation.
Then we are civilised. Say it. Say it with me. Money is . . .

Pause.

SAY IT. Money is . . .

Lulu *and* **Robbie**   Civilisation.

Brian   Yes. Yes. I'm teaching. You're learning. Money is
civilisation. And civilisation is . . . SAY IT. Don't get
frightened now. And civilisation is . . .

Lulu *and* **Robbie**   Money.

Brian *offers them the holdall.*

Brian   Here. Take it.

Lulu   You . . . ?

Brian   I want you to take it.

Lulu   It's all there.

Brian   Yes.

Lulu   Look – if you want to count it. Three thousand.

Brian   Take it from me when I tell you to take it.

Lulu *takes the bag.*

Brian   Good. Good. You see? Do you understand? I am returning the money. You see?

Lulu   I . . . yes.

Brian   And now – you have a question. Ask me the question. Please. Ask the question?

Lulu   Why?

Brian   If you formulate the question . . .

Lulu   Why didn't you take the money? Why did you give us back the money?

Brian   And now I can answer you. I answer. Because you have learnt. The lesson has been learnt you see. You understand this (*Indicates the money.*) and you are civilised. And so – I return it. I give it to you.

Lulu   Thank you.

Brian *gets up, moves to video player. He ejects the video of his son. Takes another video from his pocket. Places it in the machine. Pushes play.*

Lulu (*TV*)   One day we'll know what all this was for, all this suffering, there'll be no more mysteries, but until then we have to carry on living . . . we must work, / that's all we can do. I'm leaving by myself tomorrow, I'll teach in a school, and devote my whole life to people who need it. It's autumn now, it'll soon be winter, and there'll be snow everywhere but I'll be working . . . yes, working.

Brian   We must work.
What we've got to do is make the money. For them. My

boy. Generations to come. We won't see if of course – that purity. But they will. Just as long as we keep on making the money.
Not in chemicals. Not pure. Supplies aren't the best. So a kid dies. And then it's headlines and press conferences. And you watch the dad, you watch a grown man cry and you think: time to move out of chemicals.

He pauses the tape.

That's the future, isn't it? Shopping, Television.
And now you've proved yourselves, I'd like you to join us. All of you. Think about it.

He moves to the exit.

Our second favourite bit was the end. Because by then he's got married. And he's got a kid of his own. Right at the end he stands alone. He's on a rock and he looks up at the night, he looks up at the stars and he says: 'Father. Everything is alright, Father. I remembered. The Cycle of Being.' Or words to that effect.
You ought to see it. You'd like it.

Exit **Brian**. **Mark** *comes forward.*

Mark   It's three thousand AD. Or something. It's the future. The Earth has died. Died or we killed it. The ozone, the bombs, a meteorite. It doesn't matter. But humanity has survived. A few of us . . . jumped ship. And on we go.
So it's three thousand and blahdeblah and I'm standing in the market, some sort of bazaar. A little satellite circling Uranus. Market day. And I'm looking at this mutant. Some of them, the radiation it's made them so ugly, twisted. But this one. Wow. It's made him . . . he's tanned and blond and there's pecs and his dick . . . I mean, his dick is three-foot long.
This fat sort of ape-thing comes up to me and says . . . See the mute with the three-foot dick?
Yeah. I see him.
Well, he's mine and I own him. I own him but I hate him. If he don't sell him today I'm gonna kill him.

So . . . a deal is struck, a transaction, I take my mutant home and I get him home and I say:
I'm freeing you. I'm setting you free. You can go now. And he starts to cry. I think it's gratitude. I mean, he should be grateful but it's . . .
He says – well, he telepathises into my mind – he doesn't speak our language – he tells me:
Please. I'll die. I don't know how to . . . I can't feed myself. I've been a slave all my life. I've never had a thought of my own. I'll be dead in a week.
And I say: That's a risk I'm prepared to take.

Robbie   Thirty-six inches and no shag?

Mark   That's right.

Lulu   I like that ending.

Robbie   It's not bad.

Mark   It's the best I can do.

Robbie   Hungry now? I want you to try some. (*Of the ready meal.*)

He feeds **Mark** *with a fork.*

Nice?

Mark   Mmmmm.

Robbie   Now give him some of yours.

Lulu   Do you want some?

She feeds **Mark**.

Is that good?

Mark   Delicious.

Robbie   You've got a bit of blood.

Lulu   Bit more?

Mark   Why not?

Lulu *feeds him.*

Robbie   My turn.

Robbie *feeds* **Mark**.

Mark, **Robbie** *and* **Lulu** *take it in turns to feed each other as the lights fade to black.*

Faust is Dead

Author's Note

Faust is Dead was the outcome of a week's workshop in October 1996 with the Actors' Touring Company and continued to develop during a further workshop, the rehearsal period and through preview performances. The original production made use of video sequences, the physical skills of the performers, music and light.

I would like to dedicate the play to the director Nick Phillipou, the producer Hetty Shand and the actors Alain Pelletier and Pete Bailey. Although all the words in the finished play are mine, their imaginations and opinions all shaped the writing of the play.

In April 1988, I revised the play for a production with the Tuesday Laboratory, Los Angeles. This is the revised text.

A slash in the dialogue (/) indicates that the next actor should start their line, creating overlapping speech.

Faust is Dead was commissioned and first produced by
Actors' Touring Company for a national tour in 1997. The
cast was as follows:

Alain	Alain Pelletier
Pete	Pete Bailey
Donny	Andy Broadhurst
Chorus	Students from Marymount College

Directed by Nick Philippou
Produced by Hetty Shand
Designed by Pippa Nissen
Lighting by Zerlina Hughes
Music by Neil Starr
Video by Alain Pelletier

This revised version of the play was produced by Tuesday
Laboratory at the Zephyr Theatre, Los Angeles, from 23
May to 28 June 1998. The cast was as follows:

Alain	Alan Kolman
Pete	Jason Peck
Donny	Brian Newman
Chorus	Chastity Dotson, Alex Fox, Dolly Levan, Dan McKeever, Ronald Robinson

Directed by Allan Hendrick
Produced by Kourosh Gohar

Characters

Alain, *French*
Pete, *American*
Donny
Chorus

Setting: The West Coast of America. Present Day.

One

Chorus See, a few years ago I couldn't sleep. I'd go to
bed and then I got thinking about all this stuff in the world –
about the riots and the fighting and all the angry people and
all – and I just couldn't sleep. And sometimes I'd cry –
partly because I really wanted to sleep and I was mad that I
couldn't sleep but partly because of all those bad things
going on. And my mom would come into my room and be
just like so totally freaked that I was crying night after night.
'What's wrong, poops? You have to tell me what's wrong. Is
it the teachers at the school? Is one of the teachers at the
school doing bad things to you?'
Until eventually I'm like:
'No, Mom, it's not the teachers at the school. I'm crying for
the world, because the world is such a bad place.'
And Momma is like:
'I know, poops. It's bad now but it's getting better. It's
gonna get a whole lot better. We're going to live in a better
world.'
'I know, Momma.'
And so I pretended to sleep and my mom went off to bed.
And after that I taught myself to cry in a special way that
meant she wouldn't hear me ever again.

Two

TV show.

David Letterman So . . . you're here, you're in
America. And you've written a book. And you've called it
The Death of Man . . .

Alain Yes. That is correct. Yes.

David Letterman Neat title. What exactly does it
mean?

Alain Well, it's a complex thing to explain in a few
minutes.

David Letterman   Because I have to tell you right now I feel pretty much alive.

Laughter.

Alain   Oh yes, of course.

David Letterman   And it seems to me that you seem pretty much alive as well.

Alain   Yes, but I'm talking about man as an idea.

David Letterman   Uh uh / uh huh, yeah yeah.

Alain   As an idea, as a construct.

David Letterman   Madonna, have you read the book?

Madonna   Not yet, David.

David Letterman   But you're going to right?

Madonna   I've been pretty busy, David / you know that.

David Letterman   But you've read the other / stuff right?

Madonna   Sure, sure. The book about sexuality I thought was great.

David Letterman   Now, that is a surprise.

Laughter.

Three

Alain   I was invited to join the Director of Studies for a meal. Sushi, miso soup, sake. We were entertaining a potential sponsor for the department. He was a Japanese. And our potential sponsor asks me:
'What are you thinking about today? Please, I understand you do a lot of thinking and I'd like to know – what are you thinking about today?'
What am I thinking about today?

Well, today, I am considering an example:
In 1981 a Dutch woman was on business in Tokyo, when
she met a Japanese businessman. He invited her to join him
for a meal. She read him some of her poetry. While she was
reading, he shot her. Several times. He then chopped her
up, put her in his bowl and ate her.
That is what I am thinking about today.
The potential sponsor did not like the example. He was very
angry.
And Ms Brannigan – the Director of Studies is called Ms
Brannigan – Ms Brannigan was angry also.
I had never read the guidelines. It seems no discourse within
the university should be in any way offensive to women or to
any member of a religious or racial grouping.
Ms Brannigan said that of course the incident would only
result in a warning not a disciplinary action.
But it was the last of the straws. The camel's back was broken.
And I told Ms Brannigan to go fuck herself.
And I decided that maybe I should live a little.

Four

Tatty apartment. Very late.

Alain *is sitting. Very drunk.* **Pete** *is standing.*

Pete   You wanna take your jacket off?
Take your jacket off. Relax.
See, you relax then I guess I might relax too. Okay?
Please. Allow me.

He tries to remove the jacket.

Come on. That's it. Come on.
I kind of know one of the guys, sorta know him a little, you
know? And he said that you're a producer, that you're
seeking to sign Stevie and the band. To a major label.
You do have an . . . an . . . aura . . . of . . . authority.

Sings, grunge fashion.

Got a killer in my VCR
Killer in my ROM
Killer on the cable news
Killer in the floss I use
Killer in the floss
Killer in the floss
Killer in the floss.

See? Neat words. No. Great words. Words, yeah, but also
something about the way Steve . . . like he really totally
means it, you know? Which is like totally marketable. And I
am telling you that Stevie and the band are like totally the
thing.
Just beer. That's all? Is that what you're saying to me – you
get like this with beer?
If it's beer I can taste it, okay?

He kisses **Alain** / *tastes his mouth.*

You wanna stay over? Stay over if you want.
Yeah. This a box. Or a hole. Both a box and a hole.
This is good. To talk with you like this is good. It's
interesting. For me. Because you're different . . .

He kisses **Alain**.

Different can be sexy. Sometimes.
See, one of the guys figured that you were old and uncool
enough – no offence intended – old and uncool enough to
be A and R and Stevie sort of sent out word that if anyone
was like prepared to . . . please you then Stevie could be
very grateful to that person. So, if you wanna . . .
Okay, I understand. Sleep it off. Why not?

He tries to lift **Alain** *up. Gives up.*

Good night.
'Killer in the floss
Killer in the floss
Killer in the floss.'
We'll talk tomorrow about your signing of Stevie . . .

Alain (*in French*)   Because in America, and only in
America, am I truly at home.
For me, and for so many children of this twentieth century,
it is only in America that we really believe that we are alive,
that we are living within in our own century.

Pete   Look. Hold it right there.

He fetches his camcorder.

I'm sorry. I'm sorry but I only have a little . . . so you have
to go really slowly. Slowly. Okay.

Pete *videos* **Alain**.

Alain (*in French*)   Because in America / and only in
America, am I truly at home.
For me, and for so many children of this twentieth century,
it is only in America that we really believe that we are alive,
that we are living within in our own century.
In Europe, we are ghosts, trapped in a museum, with the
lights out and the last visitor long gone.
And so I am going to America.

Pete   Because in America . . . just America . . . is . . . really
. . . home.
For me, and for children in the twentieth century (for kids?
what's the . . . it is only America (uh uh, uh, uh, uh uh) . . .
dah dah dah belief in being alive (right), living in the century
(century that we – what? – own).
In Europe, we are spooks (phantoms, ghosts, yeah),
something in a some . . . (shit, he's getting . . . shit), lights off
and the somesuch something, yeah yeah yeah yeah.

Alain   And / so I am going to America.

Pete   And so I am going to America.

Alain   And so I say:
(*in American English*)   Hi, America. How ya doin'?

Pete   Hi, Europe. America's doing . . . just fine.
America's . . . yeah.

Five

Chorus   Yeah. I know Steve a little. My friend Jose swears
Stevie worked my shift at the drive-through a few years back
and Jose says that maybe Stevie and I even shared the same
overalls. Which is amazing. Although Jose does lie from
time to time.
See, when I look at Stevie and Stevie is up there singing,
sometimes I see . . . I know this may sound way pretentious
or way dumb or whatever . . . but I look at Stevie and I see
Kurt. It is like Kurt's . . . spirit . . . yeah, yeah, teen spirit if
you will . . . that his spirit is coming back to us through
Stevie . . . who is just beautiful, okay? In a negative sort of a
way.

Six

The next morning.

Alain *asleep in the chair. Enter* **Pete** *with junkfood breakfast.*

Pete   You wanna eat?
Hey, guy, you wanna eat something?
Good for you to eat something.
Here. Here. Okay. For you.

Alain   Thank you.

Pete   You speak English?

Alain   Of course.

Pete   Okay, that's cool.
It's just . . . last night . . .
You remember last night?

Alain   Oh yes.

Pete   Okay.
And did you find the sex good?

Did you find our sexual contact a worthwhile and
stimulating experience?

Alain   Yes.

Pete   Yes, the sex was good?

Alain   Yes. The sex was good.

Pete   That's what I figured.
I figured you didn't remember a thing.
The sex was zero. There was zero sex.

Alain   Alright.

Pete   You talked good enough.
So, you're not a producer?

Alain   No. I'm sorry.

Pete   That's okay. That's what one of the guys . . . totally
dumb.
So why were you there?
You know one of the band?

Alain   The beer.

Pete   Okay.

Alain   The beer was good.

Pete   I understand.
But if you're not a producer you're gonna have to go.

Alain   I understand.

He moves to exit, turns.

What do you think about this?

Pete   I'm sorry.

Alain   I'd like you to consider this example. I want to
know what you think.
A man meets a woman.
And he takes this woman home to his apartment and he
makes love to this woman.

Pete   This is a story?

Alain   An example.

Pete   Okay. An example.

Alain   They are making love and she asks him a question. Which is:
Which part of me do you find the most . . . the most . . .

Pete   The most arousing?

Alain   Attractive. Which part of me do you find the most attractive?
And he replies: the eyes.
It is the eyes he finds the most attractive part of this woman.

Pete   Okay.

Alain   So, the next morning he leaves. He works. But all the time he is thinking about this beautiful woman, about making love with this beautiful woman, yes?

Pete   Yes. He's thinking about her.

Alain   The following day, he is woken by the front doorbell. The doorbell is ringing, so he jumps out of bed. It might be her. Maybe she can't bear to be apart from him.

Pete   Maybe she feels the same way too.

Alain   Exactly.
But it isn't her. It's the mailman. Who has a parcel for him. So he signs for the parcel and he takes the parcel into the kitchen and he realises that the parcel . . . smells.

Pete   Of her?

Alain   Yes.

Pete   The parcel has the woman's smell.

Alain   His hands are trembling with excitement, as he pulls away the packaging – he wants the moment to last, but also he wants to discover the contents.

And as the packaging falls away, a box is revealed. A cardboard box. (*indicates*) so big . . .

Pete   Like a shoebox?

Alain   The sort of box in which you might buy shoes. The sort of cardboard box that has a lid on it.
The lid is on. He waits for a moment, delaying the moment of pleasure and then he lifts up the lid.
And inside the box are two human eyes.

Pete   So, she'd . . . Right.
She'd cut out her eyes.

Alain   Exactly. She had cut out her eyes.
Which leaves us with a question. This example gives rise to an important question.
Who was the seducer and who was the seduced?

Pete   The woman with no eyes and the guy with two eyeballs in a box.
One's the seducer, one's been seduced.

Alain   Precisely.

Pete   And which one is which?
Well, that's an interesting question.

Alain   You think so?

Pete   Yeah. I think that's a very interesting question.
You think a lot about that kind of stuff?

Alain   Oh yes.

Pete   That is cool.
I think about that kind of stuff.
You wanna tell me a little about yourself?
Tell me about the guy who thinks about all that.

Alain *moves to kiss* **Pete**.

Pete   No.
It's okay.

It's not like I have a prejudice or, or a problem, you know
. . . with the whole guys thing. It's just like it's not totally me,
okay. Sure, if you were gonna sign Stevie, but otherwise . . .

Alain   I understand.

Alain *moves to leave.*

Pete   . . . How did she find the mailbox?

Alain   I'm sorry?

Pete   That's my question.
She's there in her apartment, she's taken out her eyes, say a
pair of nail scissors something like that. So okay, she's laid
everything out in front of her. The shoebox, the paper, the
Scotch tape. And I guess she's like written the address on
before she's become . . . visually impaired. So, it's all within
easy reach.
But that still begs the question:
How did she find the mailbox.

Alain   That is not relevant.
It is an example, a model. The details are not relevant.

Pete   The mailbox is a detail, right?

Alain   Yes. Just so. The mailbox is a detail.

Pause.

Pete   I don't want you to go, okay?
I want you to stay here.
You stay here but I'd feel better if you didn't do the kissing
thing, okay?
I prefer it this way.
And see, if you wanna bring anyone else back, I can do
watching, I can do recording. I just don't do doing, okay?
Deal?

Alain   She was blind. The woman was blind.

Pete   Well, sure. She'd cut out her eyes.

Alain   But you said 'visually impaired'. She was blind.

Pete   Okay, yes. She was blind.

Alain   Yes. I stay. It's a deal.

Seven

Chorus   It's happening just like they said. Whole city's blowing right apart.
Some guy smashed the window of the store and so I got myself a VCR. Latest model. Just reached in there and got myself that honey. Bit a glass in my thumb's all the suffering I had.
'Cept I get this bitch home and my momma she's like: 'A VCR? You bring me a VCR? When we ain't got no food in the kitchen? You coulda done the food store. Listen to God, he would have told you – go do the food store.'
And I'm like: 'Momma, what is the point of having food in the house when you have nothing to watch while you're eating it?'

Eight

Alain *is lying on the floor, blood on his face. Enter* **Pete** *with his camcorder.*

Pete   'What is the point of food in the house when you have nothing to watch while you're eating it.'
Got it all on tape. Guys looting shops, guys burning cars, guys burning guys.
Oh Jesus.
Come on, guy. Come on.
What has happened to you?

Alain (*in French*)   In 1981 a Dutch woman was on business in Tokyo / when she met a Japanese businessman.

Pete   No come on. Please. You have to . . . in English, okay?

Here . . . you have to . . . calm.
What happened?

Alain   . . . In 1981 in Tokyo, a Dutch woman was on
business. On business in Tokyo and she met a man, a
Japanese man. Through her business. They became
friendly, their friendship grew until eventually she ate dinner
with him.

Pete   / Okay, I don't see the rel . . . okay.

Alain   They are eating and she reveals, she tells him that
she is a poet. She writes poetry. Love poetry. She has a
poem about him and would he like to hear the poem?
Well, alright.
So he's eating and she starts to read the poem and he pulls
out a gun and he shoots her. He shoots her dead. And then
he eats her. Cuts her up and puts her in his bowl and he eats
her and as he's eating her, all the time he's declaring his
love for her. His undying love.
Who was cruel? The man or the woman?

Pete   Please. I don't get it. I'm not so good at the whole
metaphor thing.
So you have to . . . the blood is real.

Alain   It's boring.

Pete   That's okay.

Alain   It's just a thing . . .
It's a foolish thing.

Pete   That is cool.
No really.
So . . .

Alain   Just a guy, you know. Okay. Guy in a bar.
Says that he likes me.
Says that I don't say a lot of words.
And please it is so exciting the way I look and don't talk and
of course he has a place, or he has a place and it's just not
the right place for him just now, so maybe if I knew of some
place . . .

Pete   Any time you want to do that, you do that, it's cool.
You know that.

Alain   So we got here and then he attacks me. Attacks my
eyes.

Pete   Oh Jesus.

Alain   Goes for my eyes.
Until they are full with blood. My blood.
And I don't know what . . .

Pete   You got to be careful, you know that?

Alain   'This one is for Bill.'

Pete   I'm sorry?

Alain   He says to me.
I'm down and I'm bleeding and he says to me:
'This one is for Bill.'

Pete   Shit.

Alain   Please, what does this . . . ?

Pete   Fucking Jesus fucking . . .
No.
You . . . asshole fuck.

Alain   Yes. What does that . . . ?
This one is for Bill.
Does that mean something?

Pete   Well, yes, yes of course.
Of course that means something.

Alain   You know what this means?

Pete   Oh yeah.
Oh yeah. I know what that means.

Alain   So. Please . . .

Pete   Jesus, how could you . . .
How could you do this to me?

Have you no control?
What is it with you faggots that you can't fucking . . . I
mean, can't you wait or something? Ask questions maybe?
Well, fuck you.

He exits and then re-enters with a floppy disc.

Well, that's okay then. Oh thank God. Praise be.
I'm sorry. I'm sorry.
You better come with me.
Come on. Get your shit together.

Alain   You want to go . . . ?

Pete   I'm getting out of here.
We're getting out of here.
Come on. Come on.

He starts to gather together his stuff.

Look. He's gonna come back, okay? They're not gonna let
this lie, you know?
See this? [*the disc*]. Guy who attacked you was looking for
this.
This is chaos.
Only copy in the world.
See, my dad's seen the future and he knows how to give his
product the lead for like centuries into the new millennium.
Chaos is the answer.
My dad sets up his team. Hundreds of guys looking for that
nudge into chaos.
And one day, they are there. It's ready to be released on to
the market.
Except I hate my dad so bad and I download a virus in the
chaos programme.
Total meltdown.
So all he has now is shit.
And it's just me with the real thing.
Which means he hates me but also he wants to find me real
bad, you know?
So. Please.

Alain   I like this place.

Pete   Because my dad wants to be everywhere. His software in every home, on every desk. Bill, Bill, Bill. Like God, God, God.

Alain   Bill is your father?

Pete   Yeah. Bill's my dad.
I hate my dad.
You coming with me?

Nine

Car driving through the city.

Alain   Where are we going?

Pete   Dunno.

Alain   We're just going to . . .

Pete   Yeah, just gonna drive.
That bother you?

Alain   No. That's okay.

Pete   Just gonna drive and drive.
If we anticipate even a little then my dad could figure out where to find us.
My dad sees the future like a journey down a long road.
I'm like: 'Dad, you sure there's gonna be a future?'
You wanna tell me a little about yourself?

Alain   No.

Pete   When you talk, you talk very well.

Long pause.

Alain   I want to fuck you.

Pete   Yeah?

Alain   I need to fuck you. Or you fuck me.

Pete   Maybe. Okay.
I don't have a problem with that.

Alain   You want me to get out of the car?

Pete   No. I want you here with me.

Alain   You can stop the car and let me out.

Pete   No. I don't want to do that.

Alain   If I stay with you, I fuck you.
We drive somewhere. We drive to the desert and I fuck you.

Pete   Sure, sure, I understand.
If that's the deal . . .

Alain   That's the deal.

Pete   Then I guess I'll learn to handle that.

Alain   Good.

Pete   So. You're attracted to me, right?
I'm gonna be rich. Is that what you're thinking?
See, time will pass and my dad will need this [*disc*] so bad
and then I'm gonna offer it back for a sum so vast.
And I'm gonna buy so many totally real experiences.
I'm gonna keep the peace in Bosnia. I'm gonna take
Saddam Hussein out for a pizza. I'm gonna shoot pool with
the Pope and have Boris Yeltsin show me his collection of
baseball stickers.
So who are you?

Alain   I am the man who is going to fuck you.

Pete   Yes. I see that.

Ten

Desert. Night.

Alain   This is beautiful.

Pete You like it?

Alain Oh yes.
This is a very beautiful place.

Pete I guess it's okay.
I kind of prefer it on the TV.
I prefer it with a frame around it, you know?

Alain Okay.

Pete Like you know, it stretches out, there it goes, on and on – you get the point from the TV – but when you actually see it, you know . . . it's a little scary.
Excuse me, I'm gonna have to . . .

He takes out the camcorder, looks through it.

That's better.
I kind of feel okay now.
This always works for me. Some guys it's Prozac but with me . . .

Alain I understand.

Alain *starts to feel* **Pete***'s genitals.*

Pete Oh God.
You faggot scum.

Alain Yes.
That's it.
That's okay.

Pete I don't have a prejudice here.
You filthy little weenie-feeling heap of shit.
I believe in Affirmative Action.
I believe in the multiplicity of sexualities within our society.

Alain If you look through . . .

Pete Sure, sure.

Alain If you continue to look through . . .

Pete Yes. Yes.

Alain   Keep it all within the frame.

Pete   You're right.
You're right.
I can do that.

Alain   It's on TV, okay?
It's something on TV.

Pete   Yes.

Pete records **Alain** *playing with his genitals.*

Alain   Is that okay?

Pete   Yeah. That's okay.

Alain *starts to suck* **Pete** *off.*

Pete   (*TV commentary voice*)   Lost under the stars,
surrounded by the splendour of nature and the mysterious
awesomeness of Death Valley, the kid is initiated into the
strange world of the homosexual.

Alain   You don't have to speak.

Pete   I do.

Alain   Please. No.
You don't have to say anything.

Pete   I do. Okay. I do.
Make it like on TV, okay?
And I can do that, I really can do that.
But only if I have the commentary.
I need the voice.

Alain   No.

Pete   No?

Alain   I don't want you to do that voice.

Pete   Okay.

Alain *continues to suck* **Pete** *off for some time in silence.*

Pete   There goes a racoon . . . hoppity hopping through
that piece of tumbleweed.
I'm sorry.
I'm sorry.
Hoppity hop.
Quiet.
Stop it.
That commentator. He just keeps on going.
Hoppity hop. Hey, little fella, how you doing?
And if that little fella could speak, he would tell us:
'I'm doing just fine. I'm living life out here at one with
Mother Nature.'
Don't you just wish you could do the same?

Alain *turns away and spits* **Pete***'s cum from his mouth.*

Pete   Did I come?

Alain   Yes.

Pete   Really?

Alain   Plenty.

Pete   Really, that is amazing. That is so cool.
Because you know something?
I didn't feel a thing.
You wanna go back to the car?

Alain   That's not the deal. I want to stay here.

Pete   You wanna stay here for the night?

Alain   We're gonna stay here for the night.

Pete   Alright. I'll try.

He sits.
Looks through camcorder.
Doesn't look through camcorder.

Here. Here. I have a supply.

He brings out a stash of different pills.

Here, you see. This is what we do. We go through this.
You wanna go through the Nature thing?

Alain   Yes.

Pete   You wanna go through the Nature thing and you
wanna go through the Sex thing?

Alain   Yes. Both.

Pete   Okay.
So now we are going to have an experience. Which is fine.
But just by themselves, on their own, okay, experiences
don't have a shape.
They don't have a shape and they don't have a rhythm.
And without shape, without rhythm, the experience can be
too much. It can be too painful.
So we shape the experience.
Like this.

Pete *arranges the pills in a circle around them.*

Alain   We don't have to decide the shape. We don't have
to know in advance: this one will take me up, this one will
take me down, this one will be spacey, this one will bring it
all into focus.
Let's not do that.
We'll just do them at random and allow the shape to
emerge.
You understand?

He closes his eyes, spins around, chooses a pill and takes it.

And now you.

They repeat the same process and **Pete** *takes a pill.*

Do you know what you want?

Pete   No.

Alain   But you want to find out?

Pete   Yeah. I wanna find out.

Alain   I don't want any limits, you understand?

Pete   I understand.

Alain   And how does this make you feel?

Pete   I don't know.

Alain   Scared?

Pete   Yes, scared. And, and . . .

Alain   Excited?

Pete   Excited also. Yes.

They kiss.

Alain   Man is dead, you know.
And Progress. Progress also. Progress is dead.
And Humanity. Yes. Humanity is dead.

Pete   So we're free, right?

Alain   I'm going to fuck you.

Pete   I know.
You feel anything yet?

Alain   Yes. I think it's starting.

Alain *fucks* **Pete**.

Eleven

Motel chalet. **Alain** *sits watching TV.*

Pete   I asked the guy.
I asked the guy and he said that he had plenty of other chalets.

Alain   Is that so?

Pete   Yeah. They have plenty of chalets.
You see that.
It's quiet around here, you know?

Alain   Better than the desert.

Pete   Better than the desert for that whole no people
thing.
So if you wanted another chalet . . .

Alain   You think I should have another chalet?

Pete   Yeah. That's what I'm saying. If you wanted maybe
like your own chalet.

Alain   I don't want my own chalet.
I'm fine. This is fine.

Pete   Yeah, but I think . . .
I think you should have your own chalet.

Alain   You do?

Pete   Wouldn't you like that?

Alain   No. I wouldn't like that.

Pete   You wouldn't like your own chalet?
It's what I'd like. I'd like for you to have your own chalet.

Alain   No.

Pete   Because . . . ?

Alain   Because I want to be with you.

Pete   Because you want to be with me?
Fine, okay, but I don't want to be with you.
You see? You understand?
Okay, we had an experience. Fine. That's cool. Thank you.
There, see. I'm grateful. We shared an experience. I did a
lot of new stuff. I was scared but we got through it . . . when
we were there . . . great.
But that's over . . . I'm bored.

Alain   Oh yes. Of course.

Pete   We've done it now, haven't we?

Alain   Then we'll find new things, new experiences.

Pete   I don't want that. There's no danger.

Alain   There's plenty of dangers.

Pete   I don't want you in the bed.
You're creepy.

Alain   Fine.
I'll sleep on the floor.

Pete   Is that what you want to do?

Alain   That's what I'm going to do.

Pete   I'm gonna sleep with this [*the disc*] from now on.
This is the only thing that is precious to me.

Alain   I understand.

Twelve

The next morning.

Pete   I know you. I know who you are.

Alain   Of course. Yes. You know everything.

Pete   Last night. I was cruel. I'm sorry. But I didn't know
who you were. This place sucks, you know? Sucks so bad
they don't invest in the proper channels. But what they do
have is the kind of channels that show reruns of reruns.
Like . . . reruns of old chat shows, okay?

Pete *plays a vidoetape.*

   David Letterman   So . . you're here, you're in
   America. And you've written a book. And you've called it
   The Death of Man . . .

   Alain   Yes. That is correct. Yes.

   David Letterman   Neat title. What exactly does it
   mean?

Alain   Well, it's a complex thing to explain in a few minutes.

David Letterman   Because I have to tell you right now I feel pretty much alive.

Laughter.

Pete *puts the video on hold.*

Pete   See. You see?
That's the way I know.
You gonna go back to the university? Now you lived a little.

Alain   No.

Pete   Because . . .

Alain   Because I . . . have . . . burnt my bridges.

Pete   You're so metaphorical.
What does that mean? On the TV show.
What does that mean – the End of History?
Please. I want to learn.
I want to be with you and I want you to teach me.

Alain   That means . . .

Pete *goes to fetch his camcorder.*

Alain   Without the video.

Pete *puts down his camcorder.*

Alain   I call this moment the End of History because what we understood as history, this movement forward, has ended.
And the words which have for so been our guides . . .
Progress, for example. This now means nothing.
We know this in our hearts. Every man, every woman, they know it, they feel, but they don't say it.
So we have to ask ourselves this question:
When will we embrace . . . (this is a word for you also, embrace?)

Pete Uh huh. Embrace. Yeah.

Alain . . . chaos. When will we live the End of History?
When will we live in our time?
And how will we live in this new age of chaos?
Not as we lived in the old age. Not with the old language.
Not by being more kind, more . . . enlightened.
We must be cruel, we must follow our desires and be cruel
to others, yes, but also we must be cruel to ourselves.
We must embrace suffering, we must embrace cruelty.

Pete There's a lot to learn.

Thirteen

Chorus See the minister of our church, he calls all the
moms together one day and he says:
'Ladies, we have to raise some money. We have to raise a
lot of money. Because I want the young people of this
church to be part of the future. I want them to be online.
We're going to have a terminal and a modem right here for
all our young people so they can spread the word way into
the future.'
And my mom and all the other moms worked real hard.
But when the terminal and the modem arrived they felt so
bad. Because their kids spent twenty-four-seven on the Net.
And one day they wake up and realise they are living in like
Valley of the Geeks and they never see their kids any more.
And they go see the minister. And there is wailing and like
the total gnashing of teeth. But he is just: 'Ladies, this is part
of the Lord's mystery. It may seem like he has taken your
children away, but he is working for you in a mysterious
way so let's get out there and raise those funds for more
terminals and pray for a brighter world.'

Fourteen

Pete *is on the Net, tapping at the keys.*

Enter **Alain**, *carrying brown paper bag.*

Pete   Where you been?

Alain   Walking.

Pete   You careful?

Alain   Oh yes. Very careful.

Pete   I don't like you to go out, but you go out, you be careful. They're out there.
You remember: this one is for Bill.

Alain   Of course I remember.
You wanna eat?

Pete   You shopped at a store?

Alain   Yes. A brown bag, like in the movies.

Pete   There is no need to shop at the store.
The store is a risk you don't have to take when we have a phone, we have a channel for groceries, a channel for meals . . .

Alain   I wanted to go to the store.

Pete   You go in a store, they have cameras watching you.

Alain   You gonna eat anything?

Pete   I'm not hungry right now.

Alain   What do you do on this?

Pete   I communicate.

Alain   Who do you communicate with?

Pete   Guys, mostly.
This way you get to know people, get to know people like really, really well but they don't know who you are.

Alain   Show me.

Pete   This is my space.

Alain   But I want you to show me.

Pete   Okay. For a while.
It's like . . . my own home page.

He taps on to a keyboard.

Set it up just a few days ago and now there's like hundreds
of subscribers. See . . . Coming up now . . .

An image of a teenage boy, **Donny***, on a computer screen.*

Donny   Hi, my name's Donny. How ya doing?
I've been really working on this. I want you to know that I
really used to hate my body. I used to feel so uncomfortable,
so ugly. But now I'm real happy with what I achieved. I've
been working. And I tell you: you take the pain, you get the
gain.

Donny *starts to remove his shirt.*

Pete   This guy's new.

Donny *reveals a torso that has been carefully scarred with a blade.*

Donny   Yeah. Look at these beauties. Look at that. Did it
all myself. So come on, guys, you got anything better to
show? I love these beauties, love these little babies and I'm
feeling so good. Feeling so good / about myself.

Alain   This is beautiful.

Pete   You reckon?

Alain   This is very interesting.

Pete   I guess.

Alain   He makes these marks upon himself?

Pete   Yeah. A blade, a bottle. Whatever.

Alain   He scars himself. He submits to a moment of intense . . . to a tribal agony. He creates his art. A testament of suffering upon the body.

Pete   He slices himself. Yeah.

Alain   A moment of power, of control over the self as he draws the blade through the body.

Pete   Either that or he's a loser who cuts himself.

Alain   An initiation rite for the end of the twentieth century.

Pete   Or he hurts real bad inside and he wants the outside to kinda match.

Alain   I want to speak to him.

Pete   It's not possible.

Alain   Oh yes. Communicate.

Pete   I don't think so.

Alain   You said . . . you communicate.

Pete   You don't wanna talk with Donny.

Alain   I do.

Pete   Donny is a dufus.

Alain *studies the keyboard.*

Alain   Please. How do I . . . ?

Pete   You want Donny for your collection, right? The Japanese cannibal? The woman who cut out her eyes? The dufus with the perforated pecs?
Huh?

Alain   There must be a way.

Alain *pushes a few keys.*

Pete   And what about the kid on X who fucked in the desert? Was he worth collecting or was that turning a trick?

Alain Hello, Donny. Donny – you there?

Pete Hey, listen. Listen, Donny is a fake.

Alain I don't think so.

Pete No. I don't . . . I don't believe this.
Look at this guy. It's not for real.

Alain He seems real.

Pete No, no, no. Look, look, look. See? See?
Fucking . . . ketchup . . . fucking . . . stagy fucking. Just some
fucking actress, Donny, huh? Just some fucking fake. Fuck
you. I hate that. That really gets to me.
I have to tell him. I'm gonna tell him.

Pete *types and* **Donny** *types his responses.*

Pete <DONNY, YOU ARE A FUCKING ACTRESS.
YOU THERE, DONNY?>

Donny <SURE, I'M HERE.>

Pete <DONNY, SO MANY GUYS ON THE PAGE
ARE FAKES. IT'S NOT CLEVER OR FUNNY. IT'S
EASY.>

Donny <I'M NO FAKE. I'M FOR REAL.>

Pete <NO WAY, GUY.>

Donny <WAY, GUY. ALL THIS IS FOR REAL.>

Pete <GO FUCK YOURSELF, DONNY.>

Pete Just because it's virtual, doesn't mean you can lie,
you know? Just because no one can reach out and touch it,
doesn't mean you can fake it.

Alain How did you do that?

Pete This is supposed to be real.

Alain I want to speak to him . . .

Donny   <MEET IF YOU LIKE. MEET YOU AND
YOU'LL SEE IF IT'S REAL.>

Alain   Well, how about that?
Wants to meet.
<OKAY, FELLA, LET'S MEET.>

Pete   You don't wanna meet Donny. You don't need
Donny. Donny is nothing. I'm everything.

He removes his shirt. His chest is covered in cuts.

Everything's a fucking lie, you know? The food, the TV, the
music . . . it's all pretend. And this is the one thing that's for
real. I feel it, it means something. Like suffering, like cruelty.
I did it like you said. I did it for you. You don't need Donny.

Alain   We're going to meet him.

Pete   No way.

Alain   Way. Guy.

Fifteen

Alain *and* **Pete** *are waiting.*

Pete   This is dumb. This is unnecessary.
This is dumb and unnecessary and this is dangerous.
We shouldn't be giving out details of where we are.

Alain   We can trust Donny.

Pete   You reckon?

Alain   I trust Donny.

Pete   Dufus hickety-hick sticksville retard.

Alain *picks up the camcorder.*

Alain   Please. How do I . . . ?

Pete   What are you doing with that?

Alain   I make a record.

Pete   Of Donny?

Alain   Of you. Of Donny. The cutting. 'Got it all on tape. Guys cutting guys.'

Pete   He's not gonna show most probably, you know?

Alain   I've got it.

Alain *has now worked the camcorder out and is pointing it at* **Pete**.

Pete   Hey, it's not like the guy is gonna show.

Alain   Smile. You're on TV.

A knock at the door. **Alain** *points camcorder at door and indicates that* **Pete** *should answer it.*

Alain   Please . . .

Pete   Could be anyone. Could be my dad.

Alain   Please . . .

Pete   Could be my dad's guys.

Alain *exits to answer door.* **Pete** *collects handgun from bag and waits. Enter* **Alain** *and* **Donny**. **Pete** *lowers gun.*

Donny   Hey. How you doing?

Pete   Oh, I'm . . . yeah . . . happy, happy, happy.

Pete *puts the gun away.*

Donny   Okay. You filming me?

Alain   That's right.

Donny   Is that for the network or a local thing?

Pete   It's nothing, Donny.

Donny   Oh.

Pete   It's for personal use.

Donny   Okay.
I've never been on TV.

Pete   You gotta have the face.

Donny   I got the face.
You don't like my face?

Pete   You've got a pretty face, Donny.

Donny   I knew we were gonna get along. I tried to picture what you'd be like, the both of you. Like a picture in my head. I couldn't get it so clear but all I could see was that you had kind smiles and kind eyes and we were getting on real well.

Pete   That's nice. Isn't that nice what Donny is saying?

Alain   If you keep him in the light.

Donny   Is this right? Do I look good here?

Alain   That's beautiful.

Donny   I knew I'd feel at home and I do. This feels like home already. Like you're Mom and Dad and brothers and sisters and all, just rolled into one.

Pete   Well, how about that?

Alain   Tell us about yourself, Donny.

Donny   There's not much to say.

Pete   You're doing fine so far.

Alain   Tell us about yourself.

Donny   You want me sitting down?

Alain   Whatever you want.

Pete   That's a detail. It's not relevant.

Alain   Take your shirt off.

Donny   Okay.

Pete Here.

Pete *removes* **Donny**'s *shirt.*

Donny You ready now?

Alain Oh yes.

Donny My name is Donny and I cut myself.
I had a big smile when I was a kid and my tongue was
always red and my lips were always red and my teeth were
always red. That was on account of my mom.
See, she worked nights in the store and so I'd go there after
school, hang out with my mom 'til like six in the morning
and every hour or so she'd say:
'Donny, you want something?'
'Yes, Mom. I'm thirsty.'
'What you want, Donny?'
'Want a slushie, Mommy.'
'Well, you help yourself, Donny, you go right ahead and
you take whatever you want.'
And I'd go right up to the slushie machine, press that
cardboard cup in the hole . . . and I always had cherry.
Never even gave anything else a try, because it was always
cherry I wanted. Wasn't so much as curious about the other
choices.
So, six, seven, eight cherry slushies every night your teeth
and you tongue and your mouth get pretty red.
Got so some guys called me Red Mouth Donny and some
guys who didn't know me so well just called me Red. Which
I liked.
Then one day, the slushie machine was taken away. Some
guy from the company just took it away. I think maybe the
owner of the store hadn't kept up the payments, but he
wasn't letting on.
And I felt so bad and no one could tell me why and by this
time I wasn't a kid any more. I was like eleven, twelve years
of age, but that hit me so bad.
And I started to cuss the teachers and the cussing led to
fighting with the teachers and that's when Momma said she

couldn't cope with me any more and I had to move away from her.

Saw her a few times at the hospital because they wanted to study us on account of some professor who had a theory that it was something in all those slushies that made me angry with the teachers and something in the fluorescent light in the store that gave Momma her cancer.

I reckon that's not true and those things just happened to us and that maybe if I get to ask Jesus one day he'll let me know. Jesus had quite a few cuts too by the end and I reckon he understands why I do this to myself.

I like Jesus, although I never met him. But I believe it's possible.

. . . Is that what you wanted?

Pete How many cuts you got there, Donny?

Donny I never counted them.

Pete You never counted them?

Donny I never did.

Pete You wanna compare?

Donny I reckon.

Pete Let's see who's got the most.

He takes off his shirt.

What do you think about that?

Donny You sure have got some beauties.

Pete But who's got the best? Who's the winner here, Donny?

Donny Well, I don't know.

Pete Who would you say has the most cuts here?

Alain It's the same.

Pete   Oh no. Gotta be a winner. That's what it's all about. Winners and losers. Has to be a winner. Has to be a loser. Okay?

Alain   Maybe Donny.

Pete   Yeah?

Alain   Donny has the most cuts.

Donny   Well, thank you.

Pete   Donny, I am so proud of you.

Donny   Thank you.

Pete   You wanna cut now? You wanna do that?

Donny   Sure. I can cut any time.

Pete   Alright. Let's . . . I cut first, as I lost before. Okay?

Donny   Sure.

Pete *cuts across his chest.*

Pete   You getting this?

Alain   Got it all on tape.
What do you feel?

Pete   Pure. Clear. True.
(*Hands blade to* **Donny**.) Now you. See you win this one.

Donny   I like to win. Winning's good.

Pete   Winning's good.

Donny   And I know the way. I got the way.

Donny *cuts his jugular. Collapses.*

Pete   Oh shit, man. Shit.

Alain *puts the camcorder down quickly and he and* **Pete** *rush to* **Donny**.

Alain   Stop the blood. Stop the blood.

Donny *is writhing. They try unsuccessfully to staunch the blood.*
Donny *dies.*
Everyone very still. Long long pause.
Alain *moves away from the body.*

Alain   Of course, as we look back it will become easier to
name the exact date.
Or we may never be able to say exactly. Perhaps we will
never agree a fixed point. A moment.
There will be different theories.
/ But in principle we will agree.

Pete   Quiet, please. I need some quiet.

Alain   At some point, at a moment at the end of the
twentieth century, reality ended.
Reality finished and simulation began.

Pete   Jesus. Will you . . . ?
Anyone ever tell you you talk too much?

Pause.

Alain   For myself, I would suggest fifteen hundred hours
on the thirteenth of August 1987.
Others may offer their own alternatives. A few hours, a few
days either side. So be it.
But there is a line, a divide and at some point (let's take my
point, fifteen / hundred hours, August thirteenth 1987 as a
working model), at this point, although few of us noticed, or
sensed that the change was taking place, it happened.

Pete   No. Stop.
Stop now.
Why do you have to?
Oh yeah . . . blah blah blah.

Alain   Reality died. It ended.
And we began to live this dream, this lie, this new simulated
existence.

Pete   Reality just arrived.

Alain   Some examples?
Before, in the old world, there was an event, a moment,
which was followed by analysis, by the writing of history. /
Event – analysis – history.

Pete   Look at him.

Alain   And now?
We analyse, we project, we predict – CNN, talk radio – we
anticipate an event before it takes place: the fall of a wall /
in Berlin, a war in the Gulf.

Pete   Look at what I'm showing you.

Alain   And the event itself is just a shadow, a reflection of
our analysis.

Pete   Look, just look at him.
See?
This happened. We were there. It was real.
This isn't eyeballs in a shoebox. The Japanese cannibal.
There's no ketchup.
This is Donny.
Donny is dead. Donny is here and Donny is dead.
Did you think this was gonna happen?
Did you know?
You had any idea, it was your duty to jump in there, to
intervene.
Why didn't you intervene?
He didn't have the experience, I guess.
Because if he's used the home page a few times . . . If he'd
just read the advice.
Chest, legs, stomach are fine. If you wanna do a vein, then
always cut across rather then up and seek medical assistance
immediately afterwards.
And don't ever do the jugular.
He should have known that.
He shouldn't have gone for the jugular.
I guess he was just keen to prove that he was for real, you
know?

Alain *kneels by the body.*

Alain   What we gonna do with him?

Pete   Jeez, I dunno.

Alain   A person, you know, there is so much.
So much skin and bone.
And brains and eyes.
What do you do with a person with no life in them?

Pete   I guess you bury them in the desert.
Chop them up, boil them, but those guys always seem to get
found out.
Hey, they have a whole crate of ice in the yard out there.
We fill the bath with ice and we put him in the bath until we
figure out what we're gonna do.

Alain *cradles* **Donny**'s *body.*

Alain   Donny, you're gonna be okay.

Pete   Donny, you're gonna chill.
I haven't got this [*disc*] and held on to it all this time for
some . . . kid who doesn't know how to use a blade to fuck it
all up for me, okay?

Sixteen

Chorus   Donny knew. Donny knew what he was gonna
do.
He told me:
'I'm heading out now for a real meeting. Had enough of just
communicating with all you guys in a virtual kind of way.
Had enough of it all just being pictures. See, some guys out
there want me to make it real. So, I'm gonna meet them.
Motel room and I'm gonna make it real. Totally real. I'm
gonna go for my jugular.'
And you know something? He made every TV show, every
talk show. Ricki and Oprah both got the same show: 'Death
on the Net'.

And Stevie, he already has a song about it. Which he has performed unplugged and is now showing three times an hour on MTV.
Which seems to say to me that maybe Donny wasn't so pathetic after all and he knew what was happening in his life and figured out a way to make something good come from it.

Seventeen

Motel room. Three days later. Empty.

Enter **Alain**. *Looks around.*

Enter **Pete**.

Pete   I sorted Donny out.

Alain   You got rid of Donny?

Pete   I got rid of Donny.

Alain   How did you do that?
How did you get rid of Donny?

Pete   Doesn't matter. Donny has gone. Donny has been sorted out, okay?
We have to go.
I've packed.

Alain   Where do we have to go?

Pete   I don't know, someplace.
Just move on.
I've cleared our traces here.
Few more minutes and we're moving on.

Alain   You don't want to stay here?
You don't want to conceal yourself?

Pete   That's not possible any more.
See, word is out. The word is out there.

They're all looking for us. They're checking each and every motel in the state and we stay here, they're gonna find us.

Alain   You want to keep running?

Pete   That's right.

Alain   All the time, you just want to keep running?

Pete   That's the only thing to do.

Alain   You can't think of another possibility maybe?

Pete   There are no other possibilities.
Now, come on, move.

Alain   No.

Pete   Don't argue with me.
I don't need this.

Alain   We're not gonna run around like this.
I have the disc.

Pete   You have . . . ?

Alain   Last night, you were sleeping.
I got the disc.
I'm staying here.

Pete *produces a gun.*

Alain   I'm staying here.

Pete *approaches* **Alain**.

Alain   I'm staying here.

Pete   You come with me.
You give me the disc.

Alain   Who was cruel?
The Dutch woman or the Japanese man?
It was the woman, the woman was cruel.
Because she understood the use of metaphor and he
understood nothing.

Pete *shoots* **Alain**.

Alain *falls.*
Pete *retrieves the disc.*
He cradles **Alain**.

Pete   I think that many people here would consider that
the Japanese guy was cruel.
Because he shot her. He ate her.
And I think that many people here would find that cruel.
And that woman, see?
She would never have found that mailbox.

Eighteen

Chorus   Looking back, now I'm an adult, I think I used to
cry at night not because the world was such a bad place.
Well, okay, not just because the world is such a bad place.
But also because I wanted the world to come to an end. Like
Armageddon or Hellfire or Total Meltdown or some such
catastrophe. And I cried because I felt so guilty because it
was gonna happen any day and it would be all my fault for
wanting it so much. But the world hasn't ended. It's going
on and on. And I keep on looking for signs that it's getting
better like Momma told me. But I can't see them. So, it
hasn't ended and it's not getting better. It's just going on, on
and on and on.
And I wonder if I should feel something about that.
But – you want the truth? – I don't feel a thing.
See, I'm the kind of person who can stand in the middle of
an earthquake and I'm just like 'whoa, neat earthquake'.
And I wonder what made me that way.

Nineteen

Hospital room.

Alain *is on a drip.* **Pete** *is reading from a piece of paper.*

Pete   Because man is dead. For so many centuries, we have believed in his existence. This thing, this construct, this thing we called man. But one day, some day in the twentieth century, he went and died. Sometime after Belsen, sometime after Kennedy, sometime after MTV, he went and died. As surely as, several hundred years ago now, God died and we trembled to live in a universe without him, so now we look around and see that man is no more.
What do you think?

Alain   Well, yes, this is . . .

Pete   Is it good?

Alain   Yes. This is fine.

Pete   Shall I carry on?

Alain   Please.

Pete   But now we see, we feel that we are no longer the subject but the object of forces, we are a confusion, a collision of . . .

A beeping sound.

What is that?

Alain   It tells me to take my pills.

Pete   You wanna get them?

Alain   No.

Pete   Okay.
So we're . . . there's . . . okay, okay, I got it . . . so the question is: How will we live our lives? For just as surely as there was a great battle between the centuries-old myth of God and and the newcomer Science, so the next millennium will see the fight between those who embrace and those who deny the death of man.
Would you say it's in any way derivative?

Alain   What would you say?

Pete   I've included examples of 'original thought'.

Alain   Then, fine.

Pete   For instance, well . . . for example, you make no references to MTV. I guess because you didn't have MTV when you wrote the book, right?

Alain   Exactly.

Pete   So that's an original thought, yes?

The beeping returns, louder and shriller.

Keeps on going, doesn't it?
It's important you take your pills.

Alain   It's nothing.

Pete   I'm joining my dad.
He's taking me on as a sort of number two. We did a deal on the whole chaos disc thing.
Because, see, I don't believe you.
Sure, I get your point. See, I can do the whole Death of Man speech thing, you know?
But where'd it get us?
It got us Donny.
And I don't want that any more.

He screws up the piece of paper.

My dad built this house.
Well, hundreds of guys built this house out of my dad's . . . vision.
And in my father's house, his vision of the future, of perfection is realised.
Well, look, you own a painting, okay?
And that painting has a mood. But some days that may not be your mood and here is this painting mooding out the wrong mood down on you, you know?
But my dad has solved the problem.
He buys the exclusive rights to like hundreds of total masterpieces and then programmes them into walls and if

your mood changes, click, whirr, the pictures change also.
And many, many other problems, he just went right ahead
and solved.
I hate my dad.
But you offer despair, you know that? And it may be true,
but it doesn't get us anywhere.
I'm sorry, I have a meeting to go to now.
I really want you to get better.
I really think you should take your pills.

Alain   I don't want the pills.
I don't want to get better.

Pete   Got you a present.

He hands **Alain** *a present in wrapping paper.*

To remind you of Donny.
See ya. Wouldn't wanna be ya.

Exit **Pete**.

Alain *opens the present.*
A shoebox.
He opens the shoebox.
Enter **Donny**. *No eyes.*

Donny   I was on the boat to heaven and my momma was
there and she told me you were going to die and go to hell.
So I came back because I didn't want that.
He's gone now. Gone to his daddy and they're gonna take
over the world.
I'm not gonna leave you. It's okay, I ain't ever gonna leave
you.
Come on now. Take your pills.

He pours water into a glass and cradles **Alain**'s *head as he feeds him
two pills.*

That's it. Okay.

Handbag

Handbag, commissioned by Actors' Touring Company, was first performed at the Lyric Hammersmith Studio, London, on 14 September 1998. The cast was as follows:

Tom/Cardew	Tim Crouch
Lorraine/Prism	Faith Flint
Phil	Paul Rattray
Suzanne/Constance	Julie Riley
Mauretta/Augusta	Celia Robertson
David/Moncrieff	Andrew Scarborough

Directed by Nick Philippou
Designed by Gideon Davey
Lighting by Simon Mills
Sound by Christopher Shutt
Produced by Hetty Shand

Characters

Ma:uretta
Suzanne
David
Tom
Phil
Lorraine

Prism
Augusta
Cardew
Moncrieff
Constance

The first production of the play doubled the characters as
follows: **Mauretta–Augusta**, **Suzanne–Constance**,
David–Moncrieff, **Tom–Cardew**, **Lorraine–Prism**.

A slash in the dialogue (/) is a cue for the next actor to start
their line, creating overlapping dialogue.

Scene One

Suzanne, **Mauretta** and **David** *waiting*.

Mauretta   I hope he's alright.

Suzanne   It's probably just a bit difficult . . . performing
. . . to order.

David   It means a lot to Tom. It means a lot to both of us.

Mauretta   To all of us.

David   And when it means so much . . . to all of us . . .
then it must be difficult to have a wank.

Suzanne   . . . A wank?

David   Alright. It must be hard to spill your love seed. /
Summon up the spirits of the ancestors of fertility.

Suzanne   I'm not saying . . . no. Just wank's a bit . . .
functional.

David   Alright.

Pause.

Mauretta   If Tom's finding it a bit difficult. . .

David   He'll be fine.

Mauretta   Yes, but if the pressure's really / blocking . . .

David   He'll get there.

Mauretta   Then maybe you / should . . .

David   No. We agreed. This is Tom's . . . I mean, I'm
right behind Tom . . . but Tom really wants to . . . I mean,
no kid wants to end up with my gene pool.

Mauretta   You shouldn't be so / down on yourself.

David   Gene swamp, really. I'm still trying to sort myself
out. Tom's more . . . sorted.

Pause.

Mauretta   Maybe we can help him.

Suzanne   A helping hand?

Mauretta   Well, I think that's David's territory.

David   I'll give it a go.

Mauretta   I mean . . . I don't know. Music or something.

David   I know, I know.

He produces a porn magazine.

This should do the trick.

Suzanne   No.

David   Might get him going.

Suzanne   No. No.

Mauretta   If it does / the trick. . .

Suzanne   I'm not having my . . . our baby is not being / conceived with some oiled-up, fake-tanned rent-a-dick porn model. I'm not having that.

David (*showing different pages*)   This one? This one? Or . . . how about? (*Porn star voice.*) Hey, Brad, my parents are away for the summer. How about / coming over and having a kid?

Suzanne   Put it away. Put it away.

Beat.

Mauretta   Go on. Give it a go.

Suzanne   Yes?

Mauretta   Yeah. Go on. If that's what it takes. . .

David   Alright. (*Porn star voice.*) Oh Brad, yeah. Give me that baby. Give it to me.

Exit **David** *with porn.*

Suzanne   I thought you wouldn't want . . .

Mauretta   Anything that works. Just waiting for the starter's orders now. My body's ready now, you know? All those little hormones rushing around screaming . . . come on, come on. We're up for it. Start the clock.

Suzanne   It's gonna work.

Mauretta   Think so?

Suzanne   I know it is.

Mauretta   How?

Suzanne   I dunno. I just . . . believe. I love you.

Mauretta   I love you.

Suzanne   Mummy.

Mauretta   Mummy.

Enter **David** *and* **Tom**.

Mauretta   How did you . . . ?

Tom *holds up a cup.*

Tom   Ta-tum. All done.

David   Got there all by himself.

Suzanne   Well done.

They all hug and kiss **Tom**. **Tom** *gives the cup to* **Mauretta**.

Mauretta   When I was a kid my dad walked out. One day he came home and he packed a bag and he stuck his head round the door and he said: 'I'm going out.' And that was it. He was gone and we never mentioned him again. But people would look at you and they'd say: 'It's not right. A mum and a dad's best for a kid. A kid's gotta have a mum and a dad.'
So they should be fucking pleased now. Because you, my child, will be doubly blessed. There's a positive glut of parents here for you. You've enough mummies and daddies that if one decides to pack a bag and move on you've got plenty to be going on with.

And we love you and we want you and we're waiting for you.

Mauretta *kisses the cup, passes it around the others who each kiss the cup. Loud music through the walls.*

Suzanne Oh God. The child abuser.

Tom Yes?

Suzanne Next door. The child abuser. We reckon he's got all the local kids in there. Chopped up.

Tom No?

Suzanne And we reckon he turns the music up really loud so you can't hear the screams.

Tom Oh.

David Joke.

Suzanne Yes. It's a joke.

Mauretta Right then.

Suzanne Right then. Here we go.

Mauretta Can't let this get cold.

Suzanne Fingers crossed.

Suzanne *kisses* **Mauretta**. *Exit* **Suzanne** *and* **Mauretta**.

Tom It's really not very conducive. Boom boom boom. What's that? (*The porn.*)

David That? Doesn't matter.

Tom Show me. Oh. Why did you . . . ?

David Just thought you might need . . .

Tom Not with that.

David Alright.

Tom No. I don't want this to be . . . that's . . . it's sordid.

David Sorry.

Tom . . . Sorry. I just want everything to be . . . You see so many kids. At the end of school, the parents come and pick them up. And I watch them from the staffroom window, and they grab hold of the kid's hand and it's: 'shut up' – swipe – 'keep your fucking mouth shut'. I mean, how's a child supposed to grow, develop and grow, when there's so much anger and, and . . . ugliness? And that's why I want . . . We can do so much better than that. We can create something calm and positive. We can do that.

Pause.

David I love you.

Tom And . . . I love you. Daddy.

David Daddy.

Scene Two

Victoria Station.

Prism, *in great distress, is searching. She carries a suitcase.*

Prism Oh . . . where? Oh where can it be?

*Enter **Augusta**, carrying a large handbag.*

Prism Oh thank God.
(*To **Augusta**.*) Excuse me. Excuse me. You've made a terrible mistake.

Augusta I don't think so.

Prism But you have.

Augusta I never make mistakes.

Prism Please – there has been an awful muddle.

Augusta Let me pass.

Prism We must sort out this confusion.

Augusta   Are you a lunatic?

Prism   I am a novelist.

Augusta   That is much the same thing.

Prism   No.

Prism *grabs the handbag.*

Augusta   Let go of my bag.

Prism   It's not your bag.

Augusta   I was warned that London would be like this. Lunatics, / brigands, vagabonds.

Prism   It's not your bag. It is my bag. This . . . This is your bag.

Augusta   Oh. Are you sure?

Prism   Quite sure.

Augusta   How can you tell?

Prism   Because they are quite different. Look. Look.

Augusta   I'm afraid looking is not one of my natural talents.

Prism   But surely you / can see . . . ?

Augusta   In fact all my talents are quite artificial. I shall use my glasses. Oh. What is this?

Prism   It is a handbag.

Augusta   A handbag?

Augusta *drops the bag.*

Prism   Don't. No. Don't. / Take care.

Augusta   An ordinary handbag.

Prism   If you have caused any / damage –

Augusta   The most ordinary handbag I have ever seen.

Prism   How superficial you are. You must think of the inside. What is inside is of great importance.

Augusta   To challenge substance over style is quite a challenge to society, is it not?

Prism (*talking into bag*)   There. There. No damage done. You are quite alright.

Augusta   Whatever are you . . . ?

Prism   The manuscript of my new novel.

Augusta   You are rather plain to be a novelist, are you not?

Prism   I don't think you should call me plain. Plain is a rather insulting word to use with someone you don't know.

Augusta   What an eejit . . . foolish person I am. I was forgetting one of the primary rules of life: insult only those to whom you have been introduced. Miss O'Flaherty.

Prism   Miss Prism.

Augusta   Prism. That is rather scientific, is it not?

Prism   O'Flaherty. That is rather Irish, is it not?

Augusta   Pray, don't talk to me about Ireland. I detest Ireland.

Prism   But you are Irish.

Augusta   Oh there are very few Irish left nowadays on account of their choosing to die in such vast numbers. If one encounters famine, they all must.

Prism   You sound Irish.

Augusta   How persistent you are. I am not Irish. Except by birth and upbringing. Which, I am sure you will agree, are of no relevance whatsoever. O'Flaherty does make me sound a little Irish but I shall lose the name O'Flaherty very soon. I shall be married before the season is quite over.

Prism   You seem very certain of that.

Augusta   It is inevitable. I am in my full bloom. I am here to live with my sister and her husband. No doubt you have heard of them. The Moncrieffs.

Prism   Colonel Moncrieff?

Augusta   There. I knew you had.

Prism   Colonel Moncrieff of Belgrave Square?

Augusta   I believe his Indian campaign was much remarked upon. To lose so many men in such a short space of time always leads to comment and medals and so forth. Yes. Colonel Moncrieff of Belgrave Square.

Prism   Then we are making the same journey. I too am going to live with Colonel and Mrs Moncrieff of Belgrave Square.

Augusta   How remarkable. No doubt you are a distant relation of the Colonel's. Oh, sister, delighted, delighted.

Prism   No, not sister. I am to be nanny to your sister's child.

Augusta   Oh. It is born?

Prism   No. But it is imminent.

Augusta   A nanny? Didn't you a moment ago tell me that you were a novelist?

Prism   I am a novelist . . . and a nanny.

Augusta   That doesn't seem quite proper. A baby and a book. That could lead to great confusion, could it not?

Prism   It could not. I am never confused.

Augusta   I am not quite sure it is proper to talk to a nanny. Particularly such a very plain one.

Prism   Plain, plain, plain. You are quite intolerable.

Augusta You understand me already. Now come. I like you a great deal and as I like you a great deal, you may carry my bag.

Scene Three

Office.

Phil *stands. Blood is running from his nose.*

Phil Fuck. Fuck. Fuck.

Enter **David** *with bowl of water and cloth.*

David Alright. If you . . .

Phil Cunt. Cunt. Cunt.

David If you sit down.

Phil Fucking cunt.

David Alright. If you sit down so I can. . .

Phil Ooooh.

David It's not so bad. Looks a lot worse than it is.

Phil It's not safe is it? Nowhere's safe when some cunt can just leap at you and . . .

David Keep still. Almost there.
There. No serious damage done.

Phil Should have been police around.

David Well . . .

Phil Should be police everywhere with cunts around like that. They should have cameras up. Watching them.

David Maybe it's just as well they didn't.

Phil They want to get that cunt on video. That's what they want to do.

David   You think so? Could be tricky. Put cameras up and you get all sorts of other cunts on video as well.

Phil   Well yeah. . .

David   Like cunts who snatch handbags from other poor unsuspecting cunts.

Phil   What you saying?

David   Nothing.

Phil   Come on. What you saying?

David   I'm saying that maybe there's a reason why you got a bloody nose.

Phil   You reckon?

David   And maybe if you snatch a handbag it's not surprising if someone runs after you and gives you a hard time.

Phil   I gave it back.

David   Wise move. He might have carried on kicking if you hadn't.

Phil   I could have handled him.

David   Of course you could.

Phil   You Old Bill?

David   No.

Phil   You gonna grass me up?

David   No.

Phil   So what you after?

David   Me? Nothing. Just . . . a good Samaritan.

Phil   You work here?

David   That's right.

Phil   You'll be in trouble. Back here after hours.

David   Oooh, I think they'll forgive me. Drink?

Phil   I've gotta go.

David   Stay for a drink. I'll raid the boardroom. Glass of wine? Beer?

Phil   Alright. Beer.

Exit **David**. **Phil** *goes over to a TV/video. Pushes play. Video starts:*

Suzanne (*on video*)   And that tea. Is that your regular brand of tea?

Lorraine (*on video*)   Oh yeah. We always have this one.

Suzanne (*on video*)   And why do you think that is, Lorraine?

Lorraine (*on video*)   I don't know. It's a family thing.

Suzanne (*on video*)   Is that an important consideration when you're shopping?

Lorraine (*on video*)   You get a taste for things, don't you?

Enter **David** *with two cans of beer.*

Suzanne (*on video*)   So, you wouldn't say you often try new products?

Lorraine (*on video*)   Do you think I'm old-fashioned?

David   Drinks are served.
You enjoying that?

Phil   Is that your job?

David   A part of it.

Phil   Ask people about tea bags?

David   Right now, we're the most sought-after team in the business.

Phil   To ask people about tea bags?

David To ask people about tea bags . . . in a completely new way. We actually go and live with the consumers of tea bags. Tea bags and air fresheners and pizzas. The full gamut of modern life. Live with them for a week, take along a video camera and video their choices, their habits and discover all the stuff statistics never tell us. Yeah. Thought you'd be impressed.

Phil Live with them?

David Live with them.

Phil Could get a bit . . .

David Strictly impersonal. Observation not relationship orientated.

Phil Still, you must think about . . . I mean, she's (*Woman on video.*) . . . she's alright, isn't she?

David Not my type.

Phil No. What's your type?

David Well . . .

Phil Bet your type's more. . .

David Yes?

Phil Bet I'm more your type.

David What makes you think that?

Phil 'Cos you're a good Samaritan with a stiffy.

David Well . . . yes.

Phil Good Samaritan. He didn't walk by. That's the one, isn't it? Didn't walk by. Got involved.

Phil *kneels down, undoes* **David**'s *flies. Sucks* **David**'s *cock. Almost instantly,* **David**'s *pager goes off.*

Phil Fucking hell. What's that?

David Pager.

Phil   I thought you were alarmed.

David   Listen . . . I've got to go.

Phil   Tea bag emergency?

David   Come on. I've got to go.

Phil   I'll finish you off.

David   No.

Phil   Can't go until I've finished you off.

David   It's really very important. I . . .

Phil   Only take a few minutes.

Phil *unclips the pager from* **David***'s trousers, sets it down some distance away from them, then unzips* **David***'s flies and starts sucking him off again. This goes on for some time. The pager beeps.* **David** *tries to move but* **Phil** *holds him in place. More sucking. The pager is still beeping.* **David** *struggles to get to it.* **Phil** *gets there first.*

Phil   Don't let it control you.

David   Please.

Phil   Be your own person. Say: this is my time and I am my own person.

David   Come on.

Phil *reads the page.*

Phil   'Labour started'?

David   That's right.

Phil   What does that mean? Labour started?

David   It means . . . it means my child is about to be born.

Phil   Yeah? Poof with a kid. Wicked.

David   So. Yeah, wicked. I ought to / go to the hospital.

Phil   I wasn't there. My kid was born. I wasn't there. Her mother was in another hostel. They never told me. She should have told me but she's a junkie cunt.

David   Did you want to be there?

Phil   Best to keep away. Do you want to be there?

David   Yes.

Phil   I can't even take care of myself. I can't work it out. There's so much to do, isn't there? You've got to clean yourself, your clothes, your room. You've gotta buy things and pay for things and order things. All this stuff just to take care of yourself. I mean, I can't see how anyone does it. I just can't cope. How do you cope?

David   I don't know. It's just natural.

Phil   For you. Yes. For people like you. But for me . . . I mean I cut myself. In the bathroom or the kitchen or whatever. All the time these little cuts. And I look down at it, at the blood and that and I think: I should do something about this. I should . . . it should be natural to know what to do. But I can't remember or maybe I never knew. So I just stand there. Watch myself bleeding.

David   Sort yourself out.

Phil   I'm trying, you know. I try. But things just keep on fucking up.

David   Then try harder.

Phil   I wet myself. I wet the bed. Every night I wake myself up with it and I don't know what to do and I lie in it.

David   That's disgusting.

Phil   I know.

David   Get a doctor. Get a social worker.

Phil   Get a life.

David   Yeah. Get a life.

Phil   Oh oh oh. I've done it. I've pissed myself.

David   Stop it. Stop that.

Phil   Please. Please. Help me.

David   Clean yourself up.

Phil   I don't know how. Please. Please. Don't want to be like this. Damp and pissy. You gotta. . .

David   Come on then. Alright. Alright.

David *removes* **Phil***'s trousers and mops him down.*

Phil   Has it gone now? Did you make it go away?

David   Yes. All gone now.

Phil   You're clever. I like you. See, I need you. What do you do with this? [*The cloth.*]

David   You wash it.

Phil   How do you do that then?

Beat.

Do you want me to finish you off?

David   . . .Yes.

Phil   Yes *please*.

David   Yes please.

Phil   Twenty quid.

David   I'm sorry?

Phil   Twenty quid. Come on. Nothing's for nothing. Twenty quid.

Scene Four

Flat.

Suzanne *videos* **Lorraine**, *who is eating.*

Suzanne   So what's that, Lorraine?

Lorraine   It's a pizza.

Suzanne   What type of . . . ?

Lorraine   Cheese and tomato pizza.

Suzanne   A cheese and tomato pizza.

Lorraine   Want some?

Suzanne   No thank you.

Lorraine   If you want a bit . . .

Suzanne   No thank you.

Lorraine   Is that 'getting involved'?

Suzanne   . . . That's right.

Lorraine   You're not allowed to do that, are you?

Suzanne   There doesn't seem to be . . . I can't see very much cheese.

Lorraine   You oughtta eat something.

Suzanne   In fact, I can't see any cheese at all.

Lorraine   That's right.

Suzanne   So . . . a cheese and tomato pizza with no cheese. That's a bit unusual.

Lorraine   There was cheese.

Suzanne   Yes?

Lorraine   But I scraped it off.

Suzanne   I see. / Scraped it off.

Lorraine   Yeah. Scraped it off. Go on. Taste it. It's nice.

Suzanne   Why did you scrape it off, Lorraine? Don't you
/ like the cheese?

Lorraine   You'll waste away, you will.

Suzanne   Why did you buy a cheese and tomato pizza
and scrape off the cheese?

Lorraine   Do you think I'm weird?

Suzanne   I'm not here to pass judgement.

Lorraine   You think I'm weird.

Suzanne   No, no, no.

Lorraine   You think it's stupid, scrape off the cheese.

Suzanne   No.

Lorraine   Taste it.

Suzanne   . . . No.

Lorraine   Maybe it is stupid.

Suzanne   Hey, we're all a bit stupid sometimes.
Sometimes I'm very stupid. Sometimes I'm totally bonkers.

Lorraine   You're not.

Suzanne   I am.

Lorraine   You're not.

Suzanne   So why did you scrape off the cheese, Lorraine?

Lorraine   My mum used to scrape off the cheese.

Suzanne   I see. Your mum used to scrape off the cheese.

Lorraine   That's right.
Little bit. You know you want it.

Suzanne   Well . . . thank you.

Lorraine   You're involved now.

Suzanne   Not really.

Lorraine   Put it down [*the camcorder*] for a minute.

Suzanne   No.

Lorraine   You're always on the job you, aren't you?

Suzanne   Not always, no. Just now . . . I'm . . . I'm on the
job now.
So. Your mum used to scrape off the cheese but now she . . .
She used to but now she . . . Lorraine?

Pause.

Suzanne   Lorraine?

Lorraine   She died. Last month, she died.

Suzanne   I'm sorry.

Lorraine   Yeah, well done now, isn't it?

Long pause.

Suzanne   Lorraine . . . I'm sorry.

Long pause.

Lorraine   There's lots more in the freezer. You can have
a whole one.

Suzanne   No. Thank you.

Lorraine   Alright then.

Suzanne *comes over. Hesitates. Hugs* **Lorraine**.

Lorraine   What was that for?

Suzanne   Just because . . . I didn't mean. . .

Lorraine   It's alright. . .

Suzanne   Yes?

Lorraine   Yeah. It was nice.

Pause. **Suzanne** *hugs* **Lorraine**. *Kisses the top of her head.*
Lorraine *laughs, kisses the top of* **Suzanne**'s *head. Pause.*
Suzanne *kisses* **Lorraine**'s *lips lightly.* **Lorraine** *laughs,*
kisses **Suzanne**'s *lips. Pause.* **Suzanne** *kisses* **Lorraine** *on the*
mouth for some time.

Lorraine   I didn't mean tongues.

Suzanne   No?

Lorraine   No. I didn't mean that.

Suzanne   Oh.

Suzanne *continues videoing.*

Lorraine   . . . It's not like I ever liked her. Used to lie
awake sometimes. Used to lie awake and think: Wish you'd
die. Wish you were dead you old witch. But now . . . now
. . . I . . . I go down the shops the same time as her. I watch
her programmes. I wear her clothes. I put on her clothes
and I watch her programmes and I eat pizza like she used to
eat pizza.

Suzanne   I see.

Suzanne *puts down the camera.*

Lorraine   You don't have to stop.

Suzanne   I think maybe. . .

Lorraine   I don't want you to stop.
And if the phone goes and it's the double glazing and that I
don't say: 'No. She's dead.' I say 'speaking'. I do her voice
and I say 'speaking'.

Suzanne   Listen . . .

Lorraine   I feel so empty.

Suzanne   Listen, Lorraine, let's . . .

Lorraine   Why do I feel . . . ? It's not like I ever liked her.

Suzanne *puts down the camera.*

Lorraine   I told you not to stop.

Suzanne   Lorraine, I'm just going to . . . hold you. Nothing . . . Okay?

She holds **Lorraine**.

That's it.

Her pager goes off. She ignores it. It carries on. She gets up, reads the message.

I'm sorry. I've got to go.

Lorraine   Alright then.

Suzanne   I'm sorry. It's just. . .

Lorraine   It's alright.

Suzanne   Sorry. I know it's shitty. It's just very important.

Lorraine   That's alright.

Suzanne   No really. My . . . my baby's going to be born. Our . . . my partner. . .

Lorraine   Your girlfriend?

Suzanne   Yes. My girlfriend is having a baby. And . . . I've got to be there. I want to be there.

Lorraine   Course.

Suzanne   You going to be alright?

Lorraine   Course.

Suzanne   I'm sorry.

Exit **Suzanne**.

Lorraine (*calls*)   You left your . . .

Front door slams.

Jumper.

Scene Five

Drawing room.

Cardew (*off*)   Colonel Moncrieff. Colonel Moncrieff.

*Enter **Moncrieff** followed by **Cardew**.*

Cardew   It really is most urgent. One of my boys has been mislaid.

Moncrieff   Mislaid, Mr Cardew? How careless.

Cardew   Not through want of care. No. I am the most caring and watchful / of . . .

Moncrieff   Just so.

Cardew   My boys could not receive more attention. I am at / all times . . .

Moncrieff   Of course. At all times.

Cardew   But despite my care and attention and instruction and . . . forgive me. It has been a great upset. This morning the fencing master called as usual. Instruction was about to begin when I noticed that one of the boys was missing. I called names, I counted heads. And Eustace . . . Eustace was nowhere to be found.

Moncrieff   Eustace?

Cardew   Mr Wilton.

Moncrieff   Ah, Mr Wilton.

Cardew   The search was begun immediately. Hither and thither, high and low. Willis's, Drury Lane, the Savoy. But nothing. I am beside myself.

*Enter **Constance**, heavily pregnant.*

Constance   Mr Cardew.

Moncrieff   No, my love. This is not proper.

Constance   I thought I heard voices.

Moncrieff   You must stay in your room.

Constance   Confinement is unbearable. I am so lonely.

Moncrieff   It is your burden.

Constance   Please. For a short while.

Cardew (*to* **Constance**)   Have you seen Mr Wilton?
Didn't he visit here several times? Didn't he help you
organise a little amateur theatricals?

Constance   With great enthusiasm. I fancy he may
become a great actor.

Cardew   Eustace has a great many talents.

Moncrieff   I did not consider Mr Wilton a very suitable
companion for my wife. Did I, my love?

Constance   No. You did not.

Moncrieff   I found him to be a little too . . . effeminate.

Constance   He has grace.

Cardew   He has a little too much grace about him,
despite my efforts.

Moncrieff   In fact, I find a great many of your boys a
little too effeminate.

Constance   My love.

Cardew   I give my boys all the really manly virtues. To
throw a discus, a javelin. To wrestle.

Constance *clutches her stomach.*

Cardew   . . . I wonder . . . have you seen . . . ?

Moncrieff   No. We have not seen Mr Wilton for several
months.

Cardew   Oh. Poor Eustace. The world will confuse him.
He will be troubled. He'll be wanting me.

Constance   It has started. Oh God. It has started.

Moncrieff   Come. To your room.

Cardew   If you should see Mr Wilton . . .

Moncrieff *and* **Constance** *exit.*

Enter **Augusta**.

Augusta   Oh brother. At last.
But why don't you speak . . . ? How can you be so strange?

Cardew   I think there must be some mistake.

Augusta   Please forgive a young girl's ardent expression of emotion. I come from a nation of bog dwellers and my manners want polish.

Cardew   I don't understand you.

Augusta   This cursed brogue. I must struggle to sound English if I am to be understood. Brother, it is I. Augusta.

Cardew   Augusta?

Augusta   Am I to be treated as the poor relation? I know I have a want of means. But surely a want of means is not a hindrance in society? Want of character is the only serious hindrance and I have a very great deal of character.

Cardew   I don't know you.

Augusta   This is a blow. Not know me, Colonel Moncrieff?

Cardew   There seems to be a misunderstanding.

Enter **Moncrieff**.

Cardew   This is Colonel Moncrieff.

Augusta   Brother. It is I – Augusta.

Moncrieff   Welcome, welcome. You must forgive Mr Cardew. Such proximity to a member of the female sex is altogether strange to him.

Augusta   You should marry, Mr Cardew.

Cardew   Marry? How should I find time for marriage when I have my hands so very full.

Moncrieff   Indeed. We follow Mr Cardew's activities closely.

Cardew   Yes. I am happy to say that the activities of the Belgrave Square Society for the Discovery and Betterment of Foundling Boys from the Lower Orders are reported in all the most philanthropic journals.

Moncrieff   I was not referring to philanthropic journals.

Cardew   No? What then?

Moncrieff   Talk mainly. People talk a great deal about your activities.

Constance (*off*) *cries out.*

Cardew   Good lord. What a terrible noise.

Moncrieff   Not at all. It is the sound of labour.

Cardew   Labour? Isn't that something that happens in Manchester?

Augusta   My poor sister.

Cardew   The fecundity of our species is a constant surprise to me.

Moncrieff   For a man such as yourself it must be.

Constance (*off*) *cries out.*

Cardew   Good Lord. How do you stand it?

Moncrieff   A soldier can bear almost anything.
A great many of your boys run off, don't they? What can you be doing to them?

Cardew   I don't know what you mean, sir.

Moncrieff   Oh but I think you do, sir.

Cardew   I give my boys the father they never had.

Moncrieff   And maybe the father they never wanted.

Cardew   I must find Eustace.

Moncrieff   He will return. To a father, surely he will return.

Cardew   Please, I can't bear to mislay another.

Moncrieff   Disgusting spectacle.

Cardew   Disgusting? How so? Disgusting?

Enter **Prism**.

Moncrieff   Ah this must be the new nanny.

Prism   Good evening, Colonel Moncrieff. Prism.

Cardew   Not disgusting.

Moncrieff   Thank goodness the modern age has realised the importance of dividing up our lives. Former ages, I believe, quite muddled up the aspects. Now we men can play billiards in the billiards room, smoke in the smoking room and relax in the library. And the ladies . . . well the ladies have their own worlds too.

Augusta   Indeed. I hope you will allow me to sing one evening.

Moncrieff   And then there is the world of childhood. Which is your burden.

Prism   Yes, sir.

Cardew   I cannot allow 'disgusting'.

Moncrieff   Today a child will be born and it will be taken instantly into your care.

Prism   I'm ready, sir.

Moncrieff   As yet my wife is unaware of your arrival. In fact, as yet she is unaware that you exist at all. She has resisted all suggestion of wet nurses and nannies. She thinks

she can be everything to the child. But if in time your care is
excellent, I am sure she will come to like you a great deal.

Prism   I hope so sir.

Constance *cries out.*

Moncrieff   Anticipation. It is a dreadful thing.

Cardew   I cannot allow my good name –

Moncrieff   I shall be in the billiard room.

Exit **Moncrieff**.

Cardew   'Disgusting'. That is so unjust. When all I offer is
care.

Augusta   But still. A man cannot care for so many boys
alone.

Cardew   My boys will testify that I am always most kind.
Kind and charitable.

Augusta   You should find a companion, Mr Cardew. One
who can share your calling. A helpmate, a soulmate.

Cardew   Maybe, in time . . .

Augusta   Search and you shall find.

Cardew   I must find –

Augusta   You must find a wife. A young woman. In her
full bloom.

Cardew   No. No woman can understand my mission. No
woman can care for my boys.

Augusta   Are you in *Burke's*?

She produces a copy of Burke's Peerage.

This dear volume has been my constant companion for the
last three years. Sitting amongst those ignorant Oirish,
waiting, waiting for . . . London . . . society . . . a new name.

Cardew   Please, / let me go.

Augusta   You have a town house, I know. But a country house? How many bedrooms? Are both your parents still living? / Do you smoke?

Cardew   No. No. No. I am not at all interested in marriage.

Augusta   Oh. Then maybe my dear brother is right. Maybe there is something a little . . .

Cardew   These insinuations are intolerable.

Augusta   Then marry and prove them wrong.

Cardew   I shall find Mr Wilton. I shall find him and bring him here and he will tell you, he will tell all of you, what an excellent guardian I am. You shall hear it from his mouth.

Exit **Cardew**.

Prism   Oh dear. It seems it is rather more difficult to lose a name than you thought.

Augusta   Take care. Nanny.

Prism   This must be your last season with any hope of finding a husband, is it not?

Augusta   What would you know of marriage?

Prism   I am not very much interested in marriage. At least not while there are novels to be written.

Constance *cries out.*

Augusta   She calls. My poor sister calls.

Exit **Augusta**. **Prism** *sits. Opens her bag. Gets out her manuscript. Cradles it like a baby.*

Prism   Yes. Yes. Ssssh. Ssssh.

Scene Six

Under a bridge.

Phil *is fucking* **David**. **Phil** *pulls away.*

David   No. Don't stop. Don't stop.

Phil   Fifty quid.

David   I don't think I . . . I think you've had . . .
Luncheon vouchers? AMEX?

Phil   Gotta be cash.

David *finds some money.*

David   It's all I've got left.

Phil   . . . Alright then.

He carries on fucking **David**. **David***'s mobile rings.*

You gonna get that?

They continue fucking.

I think you better get it.

David *answers the mobile.*

David   Hello? Oh. Hi. I'm sorry. I'm sorry. What more
can I – ? I'm sorry. Well, I'm trying to get awa – yes, at
work. Look. I'm sorry. What more can I – ? Fuck you. I'm
sorry that I'm busy, okay? I'm sorry I have to work. I'm
sorry that life is so fucking complicated. I love you. I love
you – Fuck.
(*To* **Phil**.) Don't stop. Don't stop.
Oh fuck it. Fuck it.

Phil *continues fucking* **David**.

David   My kid's been born.

More fucking.

Phil   Yeah?

More fucking.

Boy or a girl?

David *stops. Pushes last-number redial.*

David   Hi. Me. Boy or a girl? Well of course I care.
Because . . . because. I care, alright? Boy or a girl? You . . .
child. Boy or a girl?
He wouldn't say.

Phil *goes to fuck him again.*

David   No.

Phil   You gotta let me finish.

David   I have to go. I should be there.

Phil   So. Wham. Bam. Thank you Dad.

David   I'm sorry.

Phil   Go on then. Piss off. Piss off. You leave me here.

David   Haven't you got a home to go to?

Phil   No.

David   Oh.

Phil   They don't let me in the hostel. I'm a handful.
You look after that kid, alright?

David   Of course.

Phil   They're gonna want someone looking over them.
That's what we all want. And do you know who they're
gonna want looking over them? They're gonna want you.
You gotta be there for them.

David   Here. My card. Call me.

Phil   Might do.

David   Well . . . Whatever.

Phil   I touch their bumps, you know, women expecting.

David   Everyone does.

Phil   But really I want to punch them. You ever want that?

David   No.

Phil   Kiss goodbye?

Scene Seven

Maternity ward. **Suzanne** *sits. Enter* **Tom**.

Tom   He's on his way. That's what he said. On his way.

Suzanne   Then I'm sure.

Tom   It just makes me so fucking angry. To miss the birth. I wanted us to share that, you know?

Suzanne   I know.

Enter **Mauretta**, *holding baby.*

Tom   What did they say? Is he alright?

Mauretta   Yes. He's alright now.

Tom   But did they check . . . ?

Mauretta   Yes. The doctor's had a look and . . .

Tom   I don't think that his breathing sounds . . .

Mauretta   It's a floppy larynx.

Tom   So what does that . . . ?

Mauretta   His larynx is slightly . . . there's a potential that his larynx may block his breathing.

Suzanne   Oh God.

Mauretta   Potentially. But it's okay. We can cope with it. They're going to train us how to deal with it.

Tom   Alright.

Suzanne *kisses* **Mauretta**.

Suzanne   Isn't she a genius?

Tom   Yeah.

Suzanne   My fucking genius.

Beat.

Mauretta   They wanted to take him away.

Tom   Yes?

Mauretta   Yes. Snatch him away. Stick a little plastic marker on his wrist and shove him in a plastic box.

Tom   Well, I suppose they know what they're up to.

Mauretta   It doesn't seem natural. When what you want to do is hold on to him.

Tom   Of course you do.

Mauretta   You don't want to let go.

Suzanne   You need to sleep.

Mauretta   Bit later.

Tom   Must be knackered.

Mauretta   Yeah. And of course they lose them all the time.

Tom   No.

Mauretta   Oh yeah. There's always someone wandering around looking for a baby to grab.

Tom   Don't think so.

Mauretta   Maternity ward. Like a magnet for all those weirdos who want someone else's baby.

Suzanne   We'll stand guard, eh?

Mauretta   Yeah.
I had this woman on my show. Some girl took her baby.

And the hospital had it all on video. The security camera.
'Could it be someone you know?' So they showed her the
video, but you couldn't see the face because of course the
camera was in the wrong fucking place. 'I can't see the face.'
'Oh, but there's a moment when she looks over her
shoulder. Put it on freeze frame and you can catch the face.'
But it's all blurry and you can never quite make it out. She
watched it over and over but . . . They found the baby a
week later in a dustbin.

Enter **David**, *wearing a plastic mask and carrying a bottle of
champagne.*

David   'Over the hills and far away . . .'

Tom   Fucking hell.

David *takes off the mask.*

David   Present.

Suzanne   I don't think he's quite ready for that.

David   It's a boy?

Suzanne   Yeah. It's a boy. Jack.

David (*looks at baby*)   Who's a gorgeous boy then?

Tom   So, that makes it alright, does it?

Suzanne   Let's get organised. We need to . . . he's got a
breathing . . . a slight breathing problem. And we need to all
be trained. So, let's organise. . .

Tom *and* **Suzanne** *get out diaries.* **David** *gets out an electronic
organiser.*

Suzanne   How about tomorrow?

David   Tomorrow's bad for me.

Suzanne   Yes?

David   Yeah. Manchester tomorrow.

Tom   You didn't tell me that.

David   Course I did.

Tom   Do you get this?

Mauretta   Sometimes.

Tom   I get this all the time.

Mauretta   We book each other in. Works most of the time.

David   It's all a bit manic at the moment.

Tom   Meaning?

David   Meaning I've got no windows.

Tom   It's important. It . . . we all have to bond with him right from the beginning.

David   Bond. Right.

Tom   Otherwise he'll feel closer to. . .

Suzanne   Mummy and Mummy.

David   Mummy and Mummy?

Tom   Exactly. Mummy and Mummy than he does to . . .

David   Daddy and Daddy?

Tom   Daddy and Daddy.

David   Listen, I'm not sure about Daddy and Daddy.

Tom   No? What then?

David   Well, you as Daddy obviously –

Tom   And you're . . . ?

David   Uncle.

Tom   Uncle?

David   Uncle David. Sounds alright.

Tom   Uncle David who's around when it suits him.

David   No.

Tom   Uncle David who pops into the nursery for ten minutes when he gets back from the gym.

David   Look, it was your sperm.

Tom   Fuck you. Fuck you.

Exit **Tom**.

David   Fuck. What am I supposed to . . . ?

Mauretta   He's upset. He wanted you to be there for the birth.

David   I was working.

Suzanne   Yeah?

David   Yeah.

Mauretta (*to* **Suzanne**)   Managed to drag you away, didn't we?

Suzanne   I didn't need dragging. This girl. She's so . . . needy.

David   Must be pleased to have you around.

Suzanne   Maybe. Yes.

Enter **Tom**.

Suzanne (*to* **Mauretta**)   Come on. Let's get you both to bed.

Exit **Suzanne** *and* **Mauretta**.

Tom   You should have said a long time ago if you don't want this.

David   I want it, okay?

Tom   Sure?

David   Sure. I just – sometimes I feel like a bit of a tit being called Daddy.

Tom   Get used to it.

David   Yeah. I'm happy being a tit. Alright?

He holds up the bottle of champagne.

Drink?

Scene Eight

Office.

Lorraine *is waiting. Enter* **Suzanne**.

Lorraine   Hello.

Suzanne   Lorraine. This is a surprise.

Lorraine   Yeah. Hello.

Suzanne   . . . I'm in the middle of a presentation.

Lorraine   You left your jumper.

Suzanne   Did I?

Lorraine   Yeah. Left your jumper at mine.
It's a nice jumper. I haven't been wearing it much.

Suzanne   I have to get back. Look . . . you keep the
jumper.

Lorraine   I can't do that.

Suzanne   Course you can.

Lorraine   No.

Suzanne   I want you to have it.

Lorraine   Alright. Thanks.

Suzanne   And now I have to . . .

Lorraine   I want to speak to you.

Suzanne   I'm busy.

Lorraine I need to speak to you.

Suzanne How about a taxi? Shall we send you back in a taxi? That would be a treat.

Lorraine Don't talk to me like I'm a kid.

Suzanne I'm not. I'm just . . .

Lorraine Yeah. Yeah. Don't you fucking talk to me like I'm a . . . don't you patronise me.

Suzanne I'm not. I've just got to –

Enter **David**.

David I'm sorry.

Suzanne Lorraine, this is David.

Lorraine Hello.

David Well of course. I recognised you.

Lorraine Yeah?

David From your appearances on the television. With the pizza.

Lorraine *bursts into tears.*

Suzanne Lorraine . . .

Suzanne *is unsure what to do. After a while,* **David** *puts an arm around* **Lorraine**.

David Come on, Lorraine.

Lorraine She grassed me up.

David What? Who grassed you up, Lorraine?

Lorraine She did. She did. Suzanne . . .

Suzanne What? What?

Lorraine She grassed me up.

Suzanne Oh come on . . .

David   What do you mean, Lorraine?

Lorraine   Told the council that I shouldn't be living there.

Suzanne   No.

Lorraine   Don't fucking lie. She's lying.

Suzanne   Why would I lie, Lorraine?

Lorraine   You answered the phone. You spoke to them. 'Maggie? No one here called Maggie.' Don't say you didn't.

Suzanne   Well maybe I . . .

Lorraine   Yeah, yeah. And now I've lost it. I've lost my flat.

David   Oh dear.

Lorraine   Because that's not what you do. They call and they say 'Maggie' and I go 'speaking' and it's alright. But she . . . she . . . I've lost my flat.

Suzanne   Oh I'm sorry, Lorraine. I'm sorry.

Lorraine   Fuck all use sorry is when you've got no home.

Suzanne   But I didn't know . . .

Lorraine   No – had to go and answer the phone.

Suzanne   I didn't know you were . . . defrauding . . .

Lorraine   Fuck off . . . fuck off.

David   Hey. Hey.

Lorraine   She wanted me to have that flat. My mum wanted me to have that flat.

David   Of course.

Lorraine   Just she never put my name on the book. But I'm supposed to be there. You just go 'speaking' when they go 'Maggie'. Alright?

David   Sure.

Lorraine   So what's she gonna do about it?

Suzanne   I don't see what I can do about it.

Lorraine   You must know people. With houses and that.

Suzanne   Well . . .

Lorraine   I can get benefit.

Suzanne   No. No. I wish I could help, I wish there was a way to . . . I really . . . but . . . please, you have to go now. I have to . . .

Lorraine   You owe me. You fucking owe me.

Suzanne   I don't think so.

Lorraine   Yeah. I let you in. I told you about myself. You were nice.

David   Come on, Lorraine . . .

Lorraine   What am I gonna do? Got no mum. Got no home. What am I gonna do?

Pause.

David   You've got a spare room.

Suzanne   No.

David   Maybe for a few days . . .

Suzanne   It's not a spare room. / It's a boxroom.

David   Just for a few days until Lorraine sorts herself out.

Suzanne   There's no window.

David   Still. For a day or so.

Suzanne   It's not a good time.

Lorraine   I don't mind.

Suzanne   With the baby just . . . it's impossible to sleep.

Lorraine   I don't mind.

Suzanne   No.

Lorraine   No mum. No home.

Lorraine *bangs her head very hard several times.*

Suzanne   Stop. Stop that. Stop her.

David *and* **Suzanne** *pull her away. A scuffle.* **Lorraine** *cries.* **Suzanne** *holds her.*

Suzanne   Oh Lorraine. I'm sorry.

Lorraine   You gonna kiss me?

Suzanne   Look . . . a couple of days, alright?

Lorraine   Yeah?

Suzanne   And that's it.

Lorraine   Thank you. I'll get my stuff.

Suzanne   Lorraine, this doesn't mean . . . I don't want you to rely on me, okay?

Lorraine   Course.

Exit **Lorraine**.

David   Wooh. Kooky bitch.

Suzanne   Don't call her that.

David   Miss Kookyfuckingkookybitch. I reckon she's taken a bit of a shine to you.

Suzanne   Oh come on.

David   That's what I reckon. And I reckon you've taken a bit of a shine to Miss Kooky Bitch.

Suzanne   Lorraine.

David   Miss Kooky / Bitch Lorraine.

Suzanne   Sexist cunt.

David   Oh yeah?

Suzanne   Yeah. You are a total sexist / fucking cunt.

David   Love juice Lorraine, / I bet.

Suzanne   Fuck off.

David   Oooooh, Lorraine. Pizza? Just wait 'til I scrape off the cheese. / Munchmunchmunch.

Suzanne   Listen. I'm not the one who missed the birth, who was . . .

David   Yeah? What? Yeah?

Suzanne   All I'm saying is there may be a bit of projection going on here. That's all I'm saying.

David   Bollocks.

Suzanne   Because Mauretta and me. Solid as a fucking rock. That's what I'm saying.

David   And we're . . .

Suzanne   Maybe you're projecting on to me and / Lorraine because. . .

David   Listen, me and Tom. Tom / and me. . .

Suzanne   Bit of a glass houses scenario going on / I reckon.

David   Bollocks.

Suzanne   Oh yes? / Oh yes?

David   Yes actually talking total / bollocks out of your arse that's what you're doing. Just because I catch a glimpse . . . just because I have a bit of a laugh about you and the kooky bitch you don't have to have a go at me, right? You don't have to get the hump and start crapping on about stuff you know fuck all about. You know what your problem is, do you? Do you? I'll tell you. You've got no sense of

humour, zero. Zero. Zero. Nothing. And then you start
suggesting crap.

Suzanne   I don't think so, I don't think so. It's not me
with the wandering dick. I mean, it's not hard to . . . it's
blatant. And then you expect us to just pretend like we
haven't noticed anything. Well, we notice, alright? We
notice. We know what you're like. Somebody should tell
Tom. How can Tom not notice what you're like? That's
what gets me. Does Tom know he lives with a dog with an
itchy dick? Does he? Does he? Does he?

Pause.

Why don't you have her? Why don't you and Tom . . . ?

David   Because we're . . . me and Tom are . . . we've
decided for a trial . . . we're going to live apart for a while.

Suzanne   Oh. I see.

David   For a while.

Suzanne   Alright.

Exit **Suzanne**. *Beat. Enter* **Lorraine** *with bags.* **David** *pushes
past her to exit. Pause. Enter* **Phil**.

Lorraine   Hello.

Phil   Do you work here?

Lorraine   Yeah.

Phil   Right.

Lorraine   On and off.

Phil   I'm looking for David.

Lorraine   He's in a presentation at the moment.

Phil   Right.

Lorraine   But I can take a message.

Phil   Tell him Phil's looking for him.

Lorraine   I'll just find. . .

Lorraine *looks for pen and paper.*

Phil   I've seen you before.

Lorraine   Yeah?

Phil   Yeah. On the video. With the tea bags.

Lorraine   Oh yeah.

Phil   These your bags?

Lorraine   Yeah.

Phil   Got no home?

Lorraine   Oh yeah, but I'm going to stay with Suzanne.
They want me to look after their kid.

Phil   Like a nanny?

Lorraine   Yeah. Like a nanny.

Phil   Thought you worked here.

Lorraine   Yeah. Well, I work here . . . and I'm a nanny.

Phil   You'd be good with kids. You've got kind eyes.

Lorraine   Yeah?

Phil   Kind eyes, kind hands. Some people are just right for
taking care of people.

Lorraine   Yeah.

Phil   You tell David I'm looking for him, alright?

Lorraine   Alright.

Phil   I'll be seeing more of you.

Scene Nine

Bedsit.

Mobile rings. Enter **David**. *Answers mobile.*

David   Hello? Oh hi. What time is . . . ? Right. Oh right.
Alright. Where have you been? Right. See you in a few
minutes.

Exit **David**. *Mobile rings again. Enter* **David** *putting on trousers.
Answers mobile.*

David   Hi. Oh. Hello. Yeah? Well, it's . . . It's a bit late.
Can't we . . . ? Well, of course not. No. Why should I have
someone here? Where are you . . . ? Yeah?

He goes to window, waves.

Yeah. Alright then. See you in a minute.

He puts down the mobile.

Fuck.

Exit **David**. *Pause. Doorbell rings. Enter* **David**, *crosses, comes
back in with* **Tom**.

Tom   I thought you might have found somewhere nicer.

David   It's alright.

Tom   More of a bedsit really.

David   It's a studio apartment.

Tom   Same thing.

David   As a temporary measure.

Tom   Yeah . . . temporary measure.
Listen, I've been thinking and well . . . well, actually I've
been missing you.

David   Yeah?

Tom   Yeah. Well, actually I've been pretty fucking lost
actually.

David   Can't live with me . . . ?

Tom   Can't live without you. Fucker, eh?

David   Yeah.

Tom   So, I just wanted to say . . . with the baby and
everything. I think . . . you know, all the plans we had with
the baby . . . and it's going to be difficult, I know that. I
mean, I know I'm difficult and you're . . . well you're
absolutely fucking impossible. But if that's the way it is then
. . . yeah?

David   . . .Yeah.

Tom   Because whatever the hassle this has gotta be better
than being on your own. Being on your own's miserable.
And I don't want the kid growing up and you not being
around, okay? That doesn't seem right.

Doorbell rings.

Tom   Who's that?

David   I dunno.

Tom   Bit late to . . .

David   Nutters. Yeah, nutters or junkies from the park.
Or prostitutes. Pissed prostitutes.

Tom   Yeah?

David   Yeah. Happens all the time. Ignore them, they go
away.

Doorbell rings.

Tom   Maybe we should call the police.

David   No.

Tom   They shouldn't be doing that, middle of the night.

David   Ssssh. Pretend no one's in.

Tom   What?

David   Sssshhh.

Doorbell rings again. Pause.

Phil (*off*)   Hello. Hello.

Long pause.

Phil (*off*)   Hello. Hello. David.

Tom   He said 'David'.

David   Yeah?

Tom   Yes. He knows you.

David   No, no.

Phil (*off*)   Fucking hell. David. Come on.

Tom   Look –

David   No.

Tom   I'm going to sort this out.

Exit **Tom**.

David   Shit.

Phil (*off*)   Oh. Hello.

Tom (*off*)   Hello.

Phil   I'm looking for David.

Tom   You know David?

Phil   Yeah. Biblically.

Tom   Really? Then you'd better go through.

Enter **Phil** *followed by* **Tom**.

Phil   Hello.

David   Hello.

Phil I need a bath.

David Yeah?

Phil I smell like shit in summer.

Tom Oh, I think David quite likes that.

Phil Yeah?

Tom Oh yes, the oikier the better, isn't that right?

David Listen.

Tom Oh yes. I should just let him fuck you as you are.

Phil No.

Tom No?

Phil He likes me to fuck him.

David Oh come on.

Tom Really? He always said it hurt when I tried to do it.

David Please.

Tom Couldn't take it, could you, my love? Still, I suppose when they're pre-pubescent . . .

Phil What you saying?

Tom Nothing.

Phil You saying my dick's small?

Tom Oh, come back to me when your balls have dropped.

Phil Fuck off. Fuck off.

Phil *starts to take off his clothes.*

David Look, please. . .

Tom (*to* **David**) Come on then. You too – trousers off. Come on. Don't mind me. Trousers down and off you go.

This I have got to see. Stick his smeggy little rancid cock up you. Come on. Come on.

David   No.

Tom   Because if that's what you want. If this little piece of human garbage is all you can aspire to then fine.

Phil   Fuck off. / Don't you . . . Fuck off.

David   Please. Please. Stop.

Phil   You gonna let him talk to me like that?

David   Well I. . .

Phil   Don't you talk to me like that.

Tom   Oh don't worry. Don't you worry. I'm not going to talk to you – to you or to him – ever again.

David   Please . . .

Pause.

Phil   I'm gonna run my bath.

Exit **Phil**. *Pause.*

David   I'm sorry. I . . .

Tom   You know what? This is sad. It's just sad. It's just such a fucking tragedy when you're a grown-up and you're trying to live like you're nineteen. When all you can do is work so you can go to the gym and gossip and no pecs, no sex and live your shallow, shallow little life.

David   Yes? So what? So what do you want?

Tom   I want some kind of commitment.

David   So – up with the Wendy House. Up with the Wendy House and how did Mummy and Daddy do it and their mummy and daddy do it and let's be like them. Yeah and let's move to suburbia and / bleach those nets and twitch, twitch, twitch.

Tom   Oh fuck off, fuck off.

Exit **Tom**. *Pause. Enter* **Phil**, *a towel wrapped around him.*

Phil   Bath's running. Wanna share it?

David   No.

Phil   You can scrub all the tricky bits.

David   No. I can't handle . . . no.
I found your gear. In the cistern, I found your gear.

Phil   So?

David   So. I thought you were clean.

Phil   I am.

David   But you're still keeping your gear in my toilet?

Phil   For emergencies.

David   Yeah?

Phil   For if I have an emergency. If I can't handle stuff.

David   What stuff? You haven't got any stuff to handle.

Phil   That's what you think.

David   You've got it easy. You're safe. I feed you. I give
you clothes. If you want me to wipe your bottom . . .

Phil   I can't handle you. You do my head in.

David   Oh come on.

Phil   What you trying to make me into? What are you
doing to me? Fucking poof's food. Fucking *queen's* clothes.
That's not me. That's you that is. Well, maybe I don't want
to be you . . .

David   And what do you want to be?

Phil   I dunno . . . me.

David   And what are you exactly?

Phil   I dunno.

David   Junkie? Junkie cunt who doesn't see his own kid? Smelly little street boy druggie?

Phil   Fuck off.

David   I'm trying to make you into something.

Phil   Yeah. Your bumchum. Well, I ain't gonna do it any more. I ain't gonna stick it up you any more. Alright? Where you going?

David   I'm going to throw it away.

Phil *pushes* **David** *over, kicks him.*

Phil   What? What you gonna do that for? Fuck you. Fuck you.

David   I want you to . . . just leave me alone.

Phil   I'm not doing that.

David   I want you to go.

Phil   No. Don't go after him. Stay with me. Stay. I'm not going. I'll be here when you come back.

Exit **David**.

Phil   Shit. Shit.

Phil *exits to bathroom. Returns with his gear. Injects.*

Cardew (*off*)   Eustace. Eustace. Eustace. Eustace.

Enter **Cardew**.

Phil   Fuck.

Cardew   Eustace. Oh Eustace. You were wrong to leave me.

Phil   Yeah?

Cardew   You were foolish.

Phil   Yeah?

Cardew   I shall forgive if you will solemnly undertake never to be mislaid again.

Phil   Alright.

Cardew   You solemnly swear?

Phil   I solemnly swear. Forgive me?

Cardew   You are forgiven.

Phil   You gonna fuck me?

Cardew   Eustace.

Phil   I need a fuck.

Cardew   It's not right to talk of such things.

Phil   You've gotta fuck me.

Cardew   We can be brothers. We can be comrades. We can fight alongside each other but. . .

Phil   I'm only asking for a fuck.

Cardew   Oh Eustace. Not the gutter. The stars.

Phil   Think you can do better?

A bath appears.

Cardew   Get in the tub, Eustace.

Phil   What are you? Social worker?

Cardew   Eustace.

Phil   Don't call me that. I'm not Eustace.

Cardew   But . . . You have his face.

Phil   I'm not Eustace.

Cardew   Then I have been horribly deceived. Go. Go.

Phil   I'm not gonna go.

Cardew   Leave now.

Phil   Please. Let me stay. I'll be Eustace. I can be whatever you want me to be. How does he speak? Like this? Like this?

Cardew   He has a little too much of the aesthete about him.

Phil   Like this?

Cardew   You have him. I shall save you. You are ready to submit?

Phil   I've always wanted to be saved. But no one's offered before.

Cardew   What's your name?

Phil   Phil.

Cardew   Well, that can be changed.

Phil   Don't call me Eustace.

Cardew   Of course not. That would only lead to muddle. Two Eustaces. I wouldn't do that. Eustace will return and then think of the muddle.

Phil   So what you going to call me?

Cardew   I'll choose later, after some reflection.

Phil   So for now . . . I'm nothing. I've got no name.

Cardew   For the present.

Phil   I like that.
No clothes. No name.

He makes baby noises.

Cardew   Please. No.

Phil (*baby noises*)   Dadda. Dadda.

Cardew   This is undignified. Get in the tub.

Phil *gets in the tub.* **Cardew** *washes him.*

Cardew   We live in a sorry age. We have forgotten the
most precious teaching of the Ancients. A boy cannot reach
maturity in the family home. The family cloys. It crushes. A
boy knows this. He longs for the disciplines of the Ancients.
A boy waits for the moment. A man will arrive. An older
man. Elected by the community. One day he appears at the
family home. The mother and father tremble. They knew
that this day must come. But still it has sent a deep fear into
their hearts and they have not dared to tell the boy that this
moment will come. But now it has come. The moment has
arrived. The stranger is here.
And he takes the boy's hand. 'Come. Come with me.'
The boy turns bewildered and looks to his parents. What is
happening? Tears roll down the parents' cheeks but they
nod as if to say: You must go. You must submit.
And the stranger takes the boy and they go into the hills. A
long journey until they find a goat. And they kill the goat
and they skin the goat and the boy is dressed in the goat skin
and he drinks the goat's blood.
And he sleeps in the hills with the stranger. And every day –
a new conquest. A bison, a horse, an elephant.
Weeks later the boy goes home. And his parents are
different and he realises that they will do anything he says.
He realises that he has power. He is a man.
There. You're done. Up.

Cardew *wraps the towel around* **Phil**.

Phil   Mmmmmm.

Phil *reaches for his clothes.*

Cardew   No. These are not suitable.

A set of Victorian clothes appear.

Cardew   These are for you.

Phil   My guardian. I always knew I had a guardian.
Didn't I always say I had a guardian? My unfortunate
guardian.

Scene Ten

Drawing room.

Phil *is in the Victorian clothes. He sings a Victorian ballad as* **Cardew** *watches.*

Phil   I can't do this.

Cardew   Of course you can do it.

Phil   Alright. I don't want to do it.

Cardew   John. Don't be wilful.

Phil   I don't like John. Why do you call me John?

Cardew   Because it is both plain and becoming.

Phil   I don't want to be plain and becoming.

Cardew   You will be whatever I decide you should be.

Phil   Why can't I be called something else?

Cardew   What? Jack?

Phil   I don't know. Something else.

Cardew   They will be through in a few minutes. After three. One two three.

Phil *sings.*

Cardew   Well, it is not accurate but then anyone can sing accurately. But it is sung with great feeling, which is all that is required in polite society. The posture just a little more . . .

Cardew *arranges* **Phil**.

Phil   Why can't I stand naturally?

Cardew   Nature always benefits from a little rearrangement.

Phil   I feel uncomfortable.

Cardew　And a wilful nature must be watched at all times.
Now, I shall fetch them. We will be through shortly. The chin just a little higher.

Exit **Cardew**.

Phil　Horrid postures. Horrid chins and horrid, horrid music.

Enter **Prism** *with pram and handbag. She has a bloody nose.*

Prism　Excuse me. Excuse me. I . . .

She faints.

Phil　Fuck.

He holds **Prism**.

Come on. Come on.

Prism　Pray forgive me.

Phil　You alright?

Prism　Oh yes. Quite well thank you.

She stands, faints again. She recovers.

Oh dear.

Phil　What happened?

Prism　I have been the victim of an alarming incident.

Phil　Yeah?

Prism　Yes. I alighted, with some difficulty as I had the child in the perambulator, upon an omnibus in Gower Street which, as we turned into Bloomsbury Square, overturned, depositing me on the pavement.

Phil　Then you must be a Fallen Woman.

Prism　No. I assure you.

Phil　I've always wanted to meet a Fallen Woman.

Prism   Young man, I am quite unfallen.

The baby cries.

Phil   The child is calling for you.

Prism   Oh it is quite alright. No great damage done. Oh.

She opens the handbag.

Oh no. Oh no. Wretched temperance beverage. Cursed omnibus. Oh, what is to become of us?

Phil   What is it?

Prism   A temperance beverage, which I bought in Leamington in a moment of extravagance, has exploded in the upset and – oh, look at my manuscript. Just look at it. Maybe it can be saved. If I hurry. Please, will you wait with the baby for a while?

Phil   I can't do that.

Prism   For a very short while, while I clean –

Phil   No.

Prism   He will be no bother.

Phil   Don't leave me alone with it. Please. Please. Take it with you.

He pushes the pram to **Prism**.

Take it with you.

Prism *pushes the pram to* **Phil**.

Prism   Men are such cowards. For a moment.

Phil *pushes the pram back.*

Phil   It won't be safe. You can't trust me.

Prism   But I do. I do.

Phil   I hurt people. I hurt myself. I done a bad thing. I shouldn't have did what I did to her. I know that now.

Prism   Please. My manuscript is spoiling.

Phil   Listen. Listen. Somebody's got to listen.
My kid. My kid. She's five. Then. She's five. We've got it all.
Got a flat. Her mum's there. I'm there. And yeah, alright,
we've both got a habit, but we're coping, okay? We're
controlling it, it's not controlling us.
But I'm behind with my payments. And my dealer's giving
me hassle. I mean, he's supplying but he's giving a lot of
grief.
And I'm, 'You'll get your money. You'll get it.' Fuck knows
how.
And one day he goes: 'Let me fuck the kid. Quick fuck with
the kid. I'll be careful – it's not like I'm gonna split her or
nothing. Ten minutes and I'll let you off.'
And I'm: 'No. You perv, you nonce. No.'
And it goes on. Months. 'Let me fuck the kid.' 'No.'
But then he stops supplying and you hold out, you're going
fucking turkey but, you're a dad. Your instincts won't let
you . . .
Until. Yeah. Until . . .

Prism   I don't understand you. What strange words you
use.

Exit **Prism**.

Cardew (*off*)   Through here. We're all ready.

Enter **Cardew**, **Augusta**, **Moncrieff** *and* **Constance**. *They
sit and wait, looking at* **Phil**.

John?

Pause.

Cardew   John?

Pause.

John.

Phil   I'm not John. You can't do this to me. You're
fucking me up. You find someone else, alright? You looked

after me, you sorted me out. I'm grateful. But I'm moving on. You gotta find someone else.

Cardew   No. I don't want that.

Phil   You're a nice bloke. You'll find someone.

Cardew   I don't want that. I want you. I love you.

Phil   I don't want you to love me.

Cardew   I don't want to love you but . . .

Phil   I'm not like you. I can't be like you.

Cardew   Stay.

Exit **Phil**.

Cardew   John.

Moncrieff   Leave him be.

Cardew   But suppose he should escape.

Augusta   Escape?

Cardew   Please.

Exit **Cardew**. *The baby cries.*

Moncrieff   Why is the child left unattended?

Constance   I don't know.

Moncrieff   Where is the nanny? This won't do at all. Prism! Prism!

Exit **Moncrieff**.

Augusta   Unreliable creature. I knew from the moment I saw her on the platform she was not to be trusted.

Constance   How is our mother?

Augusta   Oh don't talk to me of her. I detest our mother.

Constance   Augusta, no.

Augusta   Our mother is of the sorry opinion that Ireland is a woman in spirit and that the spirit of Ireland resides in her.

Constance   Yes?

Augusta   A delusion which has led her to write many mystic speeches and much inflammatory poetry.

Constance   But still, she is our mother.

Augusta   Really, this modern mania for acknowledging one's parents after birth seems to me to be quite senseless.

Constance   You shouldn't say such things.

Augusta   Mothers should have their eyes plucked out. Blindness is a very attractive thing in a woman.

Constance   How cold you are.

Augusta   Although you of course will be an excellent mother.

Constance   Yes. This is of me. This came from me.

She picks up the baby.

Nothing. I feel nothing.

Scene Eleven

Corridor.

Phil (*off*)   Gobbledbybubblygobble. Hehhehhaa.
Go up. Go down. Go all the way up. Go all the way down.
Uh oh. Uh oh. Uh oh.
Tastic. Tastic. Tastic. Hehehahahaaa.

Baby cries. Enter **Lorraine** *putting her clothes on.* Enter **Phil** *in the plastic mask.*

Phil   Again. Again. Again. Again.

Lorraine   He wants me.

Phil   No bye-byes. No bye-byes.

Lorraine   I gotta go to him.

Phil   Tastic. Tastic. Again. Again.

Lorraine (*laughs*)   I told you no.

Phil   Tinky. Tinky-Winky.

Lorraine   You're mad, you.

Phil   Oh oh oh.

Lorraine   Bye bye, Tinky-Winky. Bye bye.

Phil   Again. Again.

Phil *grabs* **Lorraine**.

Lorraine   Off. Get off me.

Phil   Again. Again.

Lorraine   I told you. No.

Pause. **Phil** *takes off the mask. They kiss.*

Lorraine   Look. I got responsibilities.

Phil   Too right. This (*His erection.*) – this is your responsibility.

Lorraine   No. That's, well . . .

Phil   Yeah?

Lorraine   Well, that's a laugh, innit?

Phil   Oh, a laugh right. Yeah. Tubbyhaha.

Lorraine   Yeah. That's a giggle.

Phil   No. You're involved now.

Lorraine   Please. I've got a kid to look after. I don't want to let them down. I was only supposed to be here for a few days. But they asked me to stay on. 'Cos I'm good with him.

Phil   What they need you for?

Lorraine   He's needy. They're busy. He's ill. They can't cope.

Phil   They should learn to cope.

Lorraine   Come and have a look at him.

Phil   No.

Lorraine   Come on. He's gorgeous. You'll like him.

Phil   No.

Lorraine   He'll like you. I know he will.

Phil   I'm not good with kids. They don't like me.

Lorraine   You scared of him?

Phil   No . . . yes.

Lorraine   I love him. I never felt like I understood anyone before. Before, everyone I met . . . I'm talking, they're talking. But I never understood them. I always felt like a kid. But him. I understand him, he understands me. I like that.

Phil   They're gonna use you, you know that? Use you to bring up the kid then soon as it can stand on its own two feet they're gonna push you out, you know that?

Lorraine   No. They're not gonna do that.

Phil   They will. You watch. I wouldn't do that. You come with me. I'm not gonna push you out.

Lorraine   You're grown up now. You grow up and you're alone. You gotta do things by yourself.

Phil   Can't do everything by yourself.

Lorraine   No?

Phil   No. Some things you gotta do together.

*He slips his hands inside **Lorraine**'s knickers and starts to masturbate her.*

Do you like that?

Lorraine   Yeah.

Baby cries.

Phil   He's calling for you.

Lorraine   Yeah.

Phil   He can wait for a minute. Alright?

Lorraine   . . . Yeah. Where do you get those clothes?

Phil   Off a poof.

Lorraine   That's what I thought. You a poof?

Phil   No. But I used a poof. Got to use who you can until you grow up, haven't you?

Lorraine   Yeah.

Phil   But I don't need them any more. I'll get rid of them soon as I can.

Beat.

Lorraine   I've got my mum's knickers on.

Phil   Yeah?

Lorraine   I'm wearing my mum's knickers.

Phil   Does she know you've got them?

Lorraine   She's dead.

Phil   Nice.

Baby cries.

Lorraine   I gotta go to him.

Phil   In a minute.

He puts the mask on **Lorraine***, continues to masturbate her.*

I'm ready now. To be my own person. Always had something controlling me. The smack. And people. Didn't know who I was so I let people control me. But I'm past that now. I'm gonna find out who I am. Do you wanna find out who you? Not a nanny. That's not you. You're . . .

He moves to go down on **Lorraine**.

Yeah?

Lorraine   Yeah.

Phil *goes down on her. After a while, she pulls away.*

Lorraine   No. I gotta go to him.

Exit **Lorraine**.

Phil   Tubbytastic.

Scene Twelve

Boxroom.

Lorraine *is getting ready to go out. She is wearing a smart dress.* **Suzanne** *watches.*

Lorraine   What do you think?

Suzanne   Oh yes. I like it.

Lorraine   It's alright, isn't it?

Suzanne   It's great. Suits you.

Lorraine   You reckon?

Suzanne   Oh yes. You look great.

Lorraine   Like the one you've got.

Suzanne   I suppose it is – yes.

Lorraine   I saw you wearing it and I thought – That's nice.

Suzanne   Well, good . . .

Lorraine   I mean it's not yours. I bought it. But it's like yours.

She applies lipstick.

Hot-blooded.

Suzanne   Yes?

Lorraine   That's what they call it. Is your one Hot-Blooded?

Suzanne   No. I don't think so. No. Well . . . I'm sure that'll be appreciated. Hot-Blooded.

Lorraine   Oh yeah. He'll like this.

Baby cries.

I'll go / to him.

Suzanne   No, no, no.

Lorraine   I think he wants me.

Suzanne   Mauretta's looking after him.

Cries die away.

There.

Mauretta (*on baby alarm*)   Yes. Yes. Mummy's here.

Lorraine   Can you . . . ?

Lorraine *turns.* **Suzanne** *does up her dress.*

Suzanne   So how's it going? With this boy?

Lorraine   I like him.

Suzanne   And he likes you?

Lorraine   I reckon.

Suzanne   So . . . what's he like?

Lorraine   Nice.

Suzanne   Well, that's a good start.

Lorraine   Yeah. Nice. And . . . rich.

Suzanne   Rich? Really?

Lorraine   Yeah. Really rich. With stocks. And shares and that.

Suzanne   Lucky you.

Lorraine   Oh yeah. In the City. Selling and buying. On a computer screen. Tokyo. New York and that.

Suzanne   Job like that must involve quite a bit of travelling.

Lorraine   Travel, of course, yeah, travel. He's going to be a millionaire by the time he's twenty-five. He won't want me to do this much longer.

Suzanne   Maybe, we should start looking for / another nanny.

Lorraine   No, no. You don't need to do that.

Suzanne   But if you're going to be / moving on . . .

Lorraine   No.

Suzanne   No?

Lorraine   I told him . . . I persuaded him to let me stay. 'Cos I'm too attached to you.

Suzanne   Does he come here?

Lorraine   Not really.

Suzanne   Never?

Lorraine   Well . . .

Suzanne   Sometimes?

Lorraine   Of course sometimes . . .

Suzanne   Often?

Lorraine   No, not often. He doesn't like it here. He's not comfortable. He's used to . . . y'know . . . bigger. Posher.

Suzanne   I see.

Enter **Mauretta**.

Mauretta   Fast asleep now.

Lorraine   I'll look in on my way out.

Mauretta   No need.

Lorraine   Just have a / quick look.

Mauretta   Best to leave him be.

Lorraine   Alright then.

Mauretta   Actually, Lorraine, we wanted a word with you.

Lorraine   Yeah?

Mauretta   Just a quick word. Won't take a few minutes.

Lorraine   Alright.

Mauretta   We just wanted to say . . . we'd appreciate it if you didn't bring your boyfriend back here.

Lorraine   Alright.

Mauretta   And we'd particularly appreciate it if you didn't use our bed. . .

Lorraine   You / what?

Mauretta   For your sexual / activities.

Lorraine   I don't.

Mauretta   You don't?

Lorraine   No. Course I don't.

Mauretta   Because . . .

Lorraine   Because that would be wrong.

Mauretta   Yes. We're agreed. That would be wrong.

Suzanne   All we're trying to say is . . . this is a job. That's all we want to say. I know the pay's pretty shitty. But we pay what we can and we expect you to do your job.

Lorraine   I know, I know.

Suzanne   And we feel guilty.

Mauretta   Terribly guilty.

Suzanne   This room should be nicer . . .

Lorraine   I'm not complaining.

Suzanne   But that's the deal.

Lorraine   I know.

Mauretta   And we expect you to give him your undivided attention.

Lorraine   I do.

Mauretta   But you can't. If you're . . . entertaining then you can't be giving him your undivided attention.

Lorraine   I do give him my . . . I'm going now. He'll be waiting for me.

Mauretta   Wait . . . You're lying to us.

Lorraine   We're going to a restaurant. The table's booked.

Mauretta   Please. You're lying / to us.

Lorraine   Don't you call me a liar. You got no right to call me that. I don't have to listen to this. I'm going now.

Mauretta   We've been monitoring your activities.

Lorraine   You what?

Mauretta   We installed . . . there have been cameras watching you.

Lorraine *laughs*.

Mauretta   Yes. Really. There have been video /
cameras. . .

Lorraine   What do you fucking do that for?

Suzanne   He's our child. He's fragile. He has to be looked
after properly. We can't allow him to be neglected.

Mauretta   We hoped that we were just being paranoid.
That everything / was alright.

Lorraine   What is this?

Suzanne   You neglect him. He can cry. He can shout.

Lorraine   That's not right.

Mauretta   Do you want to watch it? Do you want me to
show it to you?

Lorraine   No.

Mauretta   And I can see why this has happened. It's
understandable. No girl wants to be tied to a baby for two
pounds an hour when . . .

Lorraine   It's not like that.

Mauretta   But. We'd like you to leave.

Lorraine   No.

Mauretta   We'd appreciate it if you were to look for
somewhere else.

Lorraine   No. I'm not doing that. I'm not going. I like
this job. (*To* **Suzanne**.) I bet you don't want me to go. You
don't want to lose me, do you?

Suzanne   I . . .

Lorraine   Yeah, yeah. She wants me to stay.

Suzanne   Lorraine . . . We both want you to go.

Beat.

Lorraine   She kissed me.

Suzanne   No.

Lorraine   Yes she did. With her tongue. Lezzy kiss she did on me. Big lezzy kiss.

Baby cries again.

He wants me.

Mauretta   No.

Lorraine   He's calling for me.

Mauretta   I told you no.

Mauretta *pushes* **Lorraine** *back.*

Lorraine   Fuck off. Fuck off, you cow. I'll fucking have you, you cow.

Lorraine *attacks* **Mauretta**. **Suzanne** *pulls her off.*

Mauretta   I want you out of my house.

Lorraine   You need me. He needs me. Someone's gotta be here for him. You can't do it. You're out. You work.

Mauretta   That's right. We work.

Lorraine   So you need . . .

Mauretta   We work so that he can have a future. He's got to have an education. He's not going to end up like . . .

Lorraine   What? What?

Mauretta   He's not going to be a two-pound-an-hour person.

Lorraine   Fuck you. Fuck you.

Exit **Mauretta**.

Suzanne   I'm sorry it all got . . . We're just trying . . . we have to do what's best for our son.

Lorraine   He likes me.

Suzanne   Yes. He does.

Lorraine   More than he likes you.

Mauretta (*on baby alarm*)   There. There. Alright now.
She's going.

Lorraine   And more than he likes her.

Scene Thirteen

Suzanne *is watching a video.*

Baby cries on video.

Phil (*on video*)   He's calling for you.

Lorraine (*on video*)   Yeah.

Phil (*on video*)   He can wait for a minute. Alright?

Enter **Mauretta***.*

Mauretta   No. Don't, love. Come on.

Suzanne   I want to watch it.

Mauretta   No. Come on.
Please. I don't want to watch it.

Suzanne   Then go somewhere else.

Mauretta   I'm not. You go somewhere else. I'm not
having this. This doesn't make it better.

Suzanne   So – you gonna make it better? How you gonna
do that? Come on then. Come on. You make it better.

Mauretta   Is it true . . . ?

Suzanne   What?

Mauretta   What she said, that you / kissed her.

Suzanne   No. Why should I . . . ? No.

Doorbell. Exit **Mauretta***, enters again with* **David***.*

David   Shit. Shit.
So . . . some boy helped her take the baby?

Mauretta   That's right. Her boyfriend.

David   So. Who is this boy? Did you give a description?
You know what he looks like?

Suzanne   Oh yes.

Suzanne *rewinds the video.*

Phil (*on video*)   I'm ready now. To be my own person.
Always had something controlling me.

Suzanne   Can't see his face now but. . .

Phil (*on video*)   The smack. And people. Didn't know who I
was so I let people control me.

Suzanne   In a minute you can . . .

Phil (*on video*)   But I'm past that now. I'm gonna find out
who I am. Do you wanna find out who you are?

Suzanne   There. That's him.

Suzanne *pauses the video.*

David   I see.

Suzanne   Recognise him?

David   No.

Suzanne   Seen him before?

David   No. Don't think so. Why should I have seen him
before?

Suzanne   Just your type.

David   Oh yeah? Oh yeah? And what are we saying /
here? What's that supposed to mean?

Suzanne   What are we saying? What are we saying?
We're saying that maybe / on one of your adventures . . .

David   Fuck off. I don't need this. / Fuck you. Cunt.

Suzanne   Yes, just maybe when you've been working your way across London then maybe you might have come across . . .

David   Fuck off.

Suzanne   I'm saying that maybe a father, / maybe a dad –

Mauretta   Hey come – she / doesn't – come on . . .

Suzanne   Maybe somebody who wanted to be a dad / could be putting it about a little bit less that's what I'm saying.

David   Instead of what? Videoing it all? Getting it all on tape is that what we're saying? Coming home to watch eight hours of video just so we can feel like Mummy? Is that / what we're saying?

Suzanne   I was watching out. I was watching out for him.

David   Oh, / well done. Well done you.

Mauretta   Shut up. You're adults the pair of you. You wanted to be Mummy. You said that.

Suzanne   Yeah.

Mauretta   And you wanted to be Uncle.

David   Yeah.

Mauretta   So fucking act like adults for fuck's sake.

Enter **Tom** *with food.*

Tom   I thought we should eat. You need to eat something.

David   Hello . . .

Tom   Fuck. What's he . . . What's he doing here?

David   Please . . .

Tom   I don't want him here. I don't want you here.

David   Listen. I fucked up, alright? I fucked up big time. But now I know . . . I need you. Hold me.

Tom *holds* **David**. **David** *cries*. **Suzanne** *rewinds the video. Presses play. On video:*

Phil (*on video*)   Didn't know who I was so I let people control me.

David   Oh no. Please don't. . .

Phil (*on video*)   But I'm past that now. I'm gonna find out who I am.

Suzanne (*to* **Tom**)   This is him.

Long pause.

David   He's a boy I . . . / I met a boy and he had no one and he needed to be looked after, alright? That's all it was. Looking after him. And I got attached. I shouldn't have done that. But what am I supposed to do? What am I fucking supposed to do? And I wanted to get rid of him. I should have got rid of the cunt but I was too weak. I was used. He was using me.

Tom   Boy? Destroyed / everything now. For a boy. Some boy to fuck you and you destroyed everything. I can't do this any more. Waiting for you, wanting you, forgiving you. I'm not doing that any more. I've been so weak but now. I hate you. I feel hate for you. It could have been so good. The baby could have brought us together. But you couldn't handle – had to ruin everything.

Suzanne   A boy, a boy. I knew it. I told you. Fucking around. Always got your dick up somebody's arse. Always using work, using me as your excuse because you've got the urge, because you're looking for a shag. How many times have I lied for you? How many times have I lied to Tom? You did this. My baby's gone and you did this with your itchy dick. Cunt. / Cunt. Cunt.

Mauretta   Shut up. Fucking SHUT UP.

Pause.

Mauretta   *My* baby. They took *my* baby.

Tom   Our baby.

Mauretta   My baby.

Tom   He loves me. He'll be missing me.

Mauretta   And what did you do? At the end of the day what did you actually do?

Tom   I . . .

Mauretta   You wanked into a cup.

Tom   It makes me Dad. I'm a father.

Mauretta   It makes you nothing. You're like him. You're like her. You're nothing. All of you. I had him. And I want him back. And we're going to live together, him and me and I'm going to watch him grow and I won't even tell him that you exist. And maybe you'll interview him one day, and maybe you'll teach him one day, and maybe you'll try and sleep with him one day and you won't even know who he is. He won't know you. Just me. That's all he needs.

Tom   All of us.

Mauretta   All of us? All of us doesn't work. Look at you.

Mauretta *moves to go.*

Suzanne   Where are you . . . ?

Mauretta   No. I don't want you. You go to her. You go to Lorraine. Go and kiss Lorraine.

Exit **Mauretta**.

David   I'm going to look for them. I . . .

Exit **David**.

Tom   I'm always looking after people. I hate that. Why do I always look after people? What I want now is someone looking after me.

Suzanne   Yes.

Tom   Hold me.

Suzanne   No.

Scene Fourteen

Phil *is bathing the baby.*

Phil   And so now there's three of them. The mum and the dad and the kid. And they've got a flat. Because that's important. And the mum and the dad have got a habit. But that's alright. Listen, it's alright. And there's a dealer. He's a bad man. And he wants to do really bad things to the kid. And the dad says: 'No. I'm not going to let you do that. I'm a father. No.' But the months go on and the dealer keeps coming back. 'Let me do bad things to the kid.' 'No.'
Then he stops supplying. But now he's a dad, he can fight it. He can go turkey this time and get through it.
And finally the dealer comes for the kid and the dad says: 'I'm free of you. I've got no habit and I'm free of you and I never want to see you again.' And the dealer starts to shake, and then he turns red like a furnace and then smoke comes out of his ears and he burns up until there's just a pair of shoes lying there and they're full of ash and that's the end.

Enter **Lorraine** *with food.*

Phil   There – you're done.

Phil *takes the baby out of the bath and wraps it in a towel.*

Lorraine   Cake or bread and butter?

Phil   Bit of both.

Phil *places the baby in a cardboard-box crib at the end of the bed.*

Lorraine   You're good with him.

Phil   Yeah.

Lorraine   See. I knew you would be. You're a natural.

Phil   We're doing alright.

Lorraine   Yes, you are. He's a bit of natural, isn't he, Jack?

Phil   I was thinking. Jack. I don't like Jack. That's their name for him.

Lorraine   What then?

Phil   I don't know. Something else. A name we give him.

Lorraine   You got an idea?

Phil   Yeah. Yeah. I know. I know.

Phil *picks up the baby, goes to put him in a bag.*

Lorraine   What you doing?

Phil   Just for a moment.

Lorraine   He don't like it in there.

Phil   For a moment. How long did you have him in there?

Lorraine   That was different, that was. I had to do that. To get him out. Save him.

Phil   Only take a minute.

He opens the bag.

Bye-bye, Jack. Bye-bye.

He puts the baby in the bag.

Come here.

Lorraine *goes over to* **Phil**. *They stand over the bag.*

Phil   No more past. Begin again. Begin now. Yeah?

Lorraine   Yeah.

Phil *reaches down and takes out the baby.*

Phil   Hello, Eustace.

Lorraine   Eustace? You're mad you.

Phil   It's alright.

Lorraine   It's different.

Phil   Suits him.

Lorraine   Alright then. Eustace.

She takes the baby and puts it in the box.

Night, night. Eustace. Night, night.

Baby cries.

Oh. He's gone and wet himself again. Where the nappies?

Phil   None left.

Lorraine   I thought you got more.

Phil   I forgot.

Lorraine   He needs a clean one.

Phil   I'll go and get some.

Lorraine   No. You sit there and eat your tea. I'll get them.
Back soon. Alright?

Phil   Alright.

Exit **Lorraine**. *Baby cries louder.* **Phil** *walks it up and down.*

Phil   Oh no, come on. Oh no.

Enter **Cardew**.

Cardew   Oh help me. Please you must help me.

Phil   I don't want to see you.

Cardew   Hide me. I am in great danger. There has been the most terrible talk about the Belgrave Square Society.

They say I do the most awful things to my boys. And now the barbarians . . . a crowd of the most barbaric kind has attacked us. My home is on fire and the boys . . . the boys have been taken away from me.

Phil That's what you get, you nonce.

Cardew John.

Phil I'm not John.

Cardew They are here. Hide me.

Phil No. See this? I've got a kid to look after.

Cardew You owe me this much.

Phil I don't owe you anything.

Cardew I brought you naked and alone. What is his name? Who are his parents? Can he speak? Only his own language. He hasn't learnt our tongue. Somebody must teach him to speak. Somebody must name him. I will be that person. And so I gave you everything.

Phil I took everything. So I could make myself into a person and now I'm a person, I don't need you any more. Used you to get what I wanted and now I don't need you.

Cardew No. You are nothing. Without me you are nothing.

Phil I don't want you. Go. Go.

Enter **Augusta**.

Augusta He is here. The invert is here.

She kicks **Cardew**.

Augusta Pervert. Boy lover.

Cardew John.

Augusta Do I sound Irish to you? No.

She kicks **Cardew**.

Say it. No.
No more Irish pokery. No more Miss O'Flaherty.
It was a music evening. I can sing only one song and that is
in French, which I was afraid would sound suggestive. But I
took my chances. Abandoned or no, I determined to give it
my best shot.
Now, as I'm sure you can imagine, I do not have a pleasant
voice but it carries well enough. And the Jewel Song carried
all the way to Lord Bracknell. Yes, your man Bracknell. I
have him.

She kicks **Cardew**.

Oh, contain my excitement. Oh contain my tongue.
Contain my heart.

She kicks **Cardew**.

He said: 'Your voice impressed me.'
I said: 'Volume often impresses more than beauty.'
And he said: 'How true, but so few women really appreciate
volume. They spend all their time trying to acquire more
beauty when all they require is to be a little louder.'
And so, naturally, I continued the conversation at a quite
extraordinary volume and so caught Lord Bracknell's heart.
And now I shall be Lady Bracknell and I shall have very
many children and they will all be completely English.

She kicks **Cardew** *repeatedly*.

Phil   Oh shit. Not breathing.

Augusta   Oh, Rule Britannia. Rule Britannia.

Phil   Make him breathe. Make him breathe.

Augusta   I know nothing of motherhood yet. I thought
marriage first, as happens in all the best families.

Exit **Augusta**.

Phil *shakes the baby*.

Phil Come on. Please. Come on.
(*Taking baby to* **Cardew**.) Can't you make him breathe?

Cardew No, John. Dead to me now.

Phil *shakes the baby.*

Phil Come on, cunt. Breathe. Come on.

He puts the baby down. Lights a cigarette.

Breathe – you.

He burns the baby's skin with the tip of his cigarette. It cries.

There. See. Can breathe if you try. Good.

Enter **Constance**.

Constance This is mine. This came from me. What it feels, I shall feel. Here. Here. To me. Give me the child.

Phil Yes. Alright.

Constance Oh yes. Come here. Come here. Let me feel something.

She takes the baby.

And now, of course, it should flow through me. Now I should feel overwhelmed by a mother's love.

Phil And what do you feel?

Constance Nothing.

Phil Here. Give him to me.

Constance No. It will come. Hold him long enough and it must come. Don't want to look down and see – what? – little square bundle of feet and teeth and eyes. That is not it, is it? No. No. No. Should see love. That is quite the proper thing to see. So why? Feed him. Feed him. That will do it. Yes. That will do it.

Enter **Moncrieff** *and* **Prism**.

Moncrieff Oh my love. No. No. Come.

Constance   Must do my duty.

Moncrieff   Not the duty of an animal.

Constance   Must be as one with the child.

Moncrieff   Not like this. Come.
Now – hand the child over. Cling to the child and the child
will cling to you.

Constance *hands the baby to* **Prism**.

Moncrieff   Now we will go about our business. My
billiards, your piano. And from time to time the child will be
shown to us and we will be shown to the child. And so the
proper degree of affection between parent and child will
grow. You understand?

Constance   Yes.

Moncrieff   Good.

Exit **Moncrieff** *and* **Constance**.

Prism   You were born in quite the wrong family, were
you not? Neither father nor mother to care for you. So, why
should I?

She sits and works on her novel. Baby cries.

I'll thank you for a moment's silence. Please. If I could just
enjoy a moment's silence.

Phil   Here. I'm good with him. I'll . . .

Phil *takes the baby*.

Prism   Well, that is a little better.
Really, how am I to deal adequately with fiction when
reality keeps making such rude interruptions on my time?
Because, really, you are a single infant. You really won't
make one bit of difference to the world.
Whereas this is a novel. Think of the emotion and
instruction contained in a three-volume novel and think of
the thousands of readers.

I have just reached the part where she goes into the night, out into the storm to challenge the ghost . . .

Phil   Isn't breathing.

(*Taking baby to* **Prism**.)   Isn't breathing.

Prism   I must have peace. Peace. I don't want you. Why won't someone take you away? Why won't the bogeyman or anyone take you away?

Cardew   Might I be allowed . . .

Prism   Mr Cardew. I thought they had driven you from the town.

Cardew   I will be leaving London shortly. I will begin again. I thought the coast. Worthing, I think. Nobody much bothers what happens in Worthing.

Prism   But you will still have your boys?

Cardew   If I cannot care for another what am I? But I have been too liberal with my charity, my care has been too ostentatious. Now I shall care for just one lost soul, one boy.

Prism   A child in need of care? A child ignored and forgotten by its parents?

Cardew   Exactly. Might I have . . . ?

Prism   Bags become so easily muddled at Victoria Station. It is quite possible, in a moment of mental abstraction, I should place my manuscript in the perambulator and the baby in this handbag. What a confusion. And that, similarly abstracted, you should mistake my bag for your own.

Cardew   Victoria Station? Which line?

Prism   The Brighton line.

Cardew   Thank you, thank you.

Exit **Cardew**.

Prism   To he who needs the child, the child shall be given. That is what justice means.

Exit **Prism**.

Phil   Oh no. Can't get me like that. Know how to make you start again. See I know how.

He stubs the cigarette on the baby. Nothing.

Come on. Come on.

Stubs the cigarette. Nothing. Again. Again. Again.

Come on. Come on.

He pushes the cigarette into the baby's eyes.

Just gonna be awkward? Just not gonna breathe, eh? Alright. Alright.

He sits, looks at the baby. Long pause.

He puts the baby in a bin-bag.

Enter **Cardew** *with handbag. Sets it down carefully. Opens it. Brings out a baby.*

Cardew   My own.

Enter **Lorraine** *with shopping bag. Puts down shopping bag. Goes to cradle. Sees it is empty.*

Phil   I did a bad thing. I . . .

Lorraine *goes to bin-bag, picks it up.*

Cardew   My own one.

Lorraine *cradles the bin-bag.* **Cardew** *cradles the baby.* **Phil** *howls.*

Some Explicit Polaroids

Some Explicit Polaroids, produced by Out of Joint, was first performed at the Theatre Royal, Bury St Edmunds, on 30 September 1999 prior to a run at the New Ambassadors, London. The cast was as follows:

Tim	Russell Barr
Nadia	Fritha Goodey
Helen	Sally Rogers
Nick	Nick Dunning
Jonathan	David Sibley
Victor	Matthew Wait

Directed by Max Stafford-Clark
Designed by Julian McGowan
Lighting by Johanna Town
Sound by Paul Arditti

Characters

Helen
Nick
Nadia
Victor
Tim
Jonathan

A slash in the dialogue (/) is a cue for the next actor to start their line, creating overlapping dialogue.

Scene One

Helen's *flat*

Nick *and* **Helen**. **Nick** *is very wet.*

Helen   Nick. Fucking hell. Nick.

Nick   Hello, Helen.

Helen   Fucking hell.

Nick   I tried to ring you.

Helen   You're / wet.

Nick   Wet. Yeah. It's raining.

Helen   Right.

Nick   I tried to ring you. Let you know. But I was there and I couldn't work out how to get the money in and there's a girl behind me and she says 'they only take cards' and I'm like cards? What the fuck does she mean 'cards'?

Helen   Listen, I have to –

Nick   I'm soaked. I need to change my / clothes.

Helen   Nick, I was on my way out.

Nick   I thought maybe you still had some of my gear . . .

Helen   Sorry?

Nick   Something I could change into?

Helen   Nick. I threw it all away.

Nick   What? All of it?

Helen   All of it. Years ago.

Nick   Right. Right. I see. You look smart.

Helen   I've got a meeting to go to.

Nick   Kid in the lift tried to sell me smack. Must have been about seven. I said: 'You shouldn't be selling drugs at

your age.' And he said: 'How else am I gonna buy a
PlayStation?'

Helen   There's a lot of that goes on.

Nick   What the fuck is a PlayStation? How's your mum?

Helen   Dead.

Nick   Right. Right. But the council let you –

Helen   I bought it.

Nick   Yeah?

Helen   Yes. I bought the flat from the council. Alright?

Nick   Fucking hell, Helen.

Helen   Yeah. Propertied classes me. So, what you going to
do to me? Firebomb through the letter box? Picket the
entryphone. Or maybe you're going to kidnap / me and do
all sorts of terrible things to me?

Nick   No. No. No. I've changed.

Helen   Well good.

Nick   I really want to change out of these clothes. I think I
might get flu or something.

Helen   Nick –

Nick   Maybe if I just –

Helen   I haven't got time for this.

Nick *starts to take off his clothes.*

Helen   Nick.

Nick   There's no ring. You're not / married.

Helen   No.

Nick   I think that's a good choice. Not to tie yourself down
like that. Keep your independence. Play the field a bit when

you fancy it. I think that's a really good choice you've made there.

Helen   There was someone.

Nick   Right.

Helen   For a few years but in the end she moved.

Nick   She?

Helen   Yes. She moved to America.

Nick   Really? / She?

Helen   She's in computing. I still get the odd card from Silicon Valley.

Nick   So you're a . . . ? What? You're . . .

Helen   There's been a few blokes / as well.

Nick   Right. Right. You still look great.

Helen   I look middle-aged. I am middle-aged.

Nick   No, you're . . . So, nobody actually around at the moment?

Helen   Maybe. No . . . It's none of your business actually, is it?

Nick   No toy boy in the bedroom? No lady wrestlers behind the sofa?

Helen   Yeah. But they all hid when they heard the door go. Which doesn't mean I'm up for it, okay?

Nick   I wasn't asking.

Helen   Alright. Just in case you were thinking of . . . Don't.

Nick   Alright then.

Helen   You're going to have to put those on again. I've got a meeting and I'm already running late.

Nick   Yeah.

Helen   You caught me on my way to a meeting.

Nick   What sort of meeting?

Helen   Council meeting. I'm a councillor.

Nick   Yeah?

Helen   Yes. Nowadays I'm a councillor, hence . . .

Nick   Smart clothes.

Helen   Hence smart clothes. Look. There's some jeans and a T-shirt Finnoula left. She was quite a big girl. You can have them.

Nick   I need somewhere to stay.

Helen   Oh.

Nick   I'm sort of stuck and I need somewhere to stay and I thought you might just put me up until . . .

Helen   I'm sorry, Nick.

Nick   For a short time.

Helen   No.

Nick   Why?

Helen   Because I don't want to. Because I don't want you here.

Nick   I did it for you.

Helen   Fuck off.

Nick   I did it because you wanted me to.

Helen   What is this bollocks? This is bollocks.

Nick   You said: 'That bastard is the scum of the earth and someone should kill that bastard.'

Helen   We all said that stuff. We said rubbish / like that all the time.

Nick I'm not blaming . . . Listen. Your dad, when they laid off your dad, when that bastard buys it up and they're gonna asset-strip, chuck your dad away and you wanted him dead.

Helen I was twenty. Everyone was a fascist or a scab or a class traitor. 'Eat the rich.' We used to chant that, I mean what the fuck did that mean – 'eat the rich'?

Nick And you said to me . . . 'He should be killed.'

Helen Did I?

Nick Yes.

Helen Then I was very stupid.

Nick And I said: 'I'll do it.'

Helen I don't remember. Because I can't imagine that I ever thought –

Nick It was real for me. Scab, class traitor. I wasn't playing.

Helen Yeah, well, we all thought it was real at the time. At the time, we all believed it. Do you still believe it?

Nick I've only just got out. I don't understand anything now.

Helen Well, everything's changed.

Nick And you've changed?

Helen Of course. Look at me.

Nick Let me stay.

Helen No.

Nick Looking at you now, I still feel a lot of the same stuff. About you.

Helen You're looking at a different person.

Nick Same feelings.

Helen   Yeah?

Nick   Yeah. And what are you feeling right now?

Helen   I don't know.

Nick   A few of the old feelings?

Helen   Maybe . . . Yes, a few of the old feelings.

Nick   A couple of days.

Helen   . . . Okay.

Nick   I want to learn . . . I want to understand how the world works now.

Helen   Don't ask me. You start with the little stuff . . . Okay?

Nick   Alright.

Helen   Bit by bit, you do what you can and you don't look for the bigger picture, you don't generalise.

Nick   You were always a good teacher.

Helen   Yeah?

Nick   Yeah. You taught me a lot of stuff.

Helen   What kind of stuff?

Nick   All sorts of stuff.

They kiss.

Of course I'm a bit rusty on a few things. I need a bit of revision.

Helen   Then you sit here and revise on your own.

Nick   There's a word for that.

Helen   I wouldn't know.

Nick   That's all you get in prison.

Helen   That's all you're getting here.

Nick   That's a shame.

Helen   I've got to go now. I'll see you later.

Nick   And what's your meeting about, councillor?

Helen   Boring stuff.

Nick   Go on.

Helen   It's nothing . . . Boring stuff.

Nick   Tell me. Tell me.

Helen   It's bus companies. They've deregulated the buses and now there's hundreds of different buses whizzing around and the whole thing's a mess and I'm trying to co-ordinate . . .

Nick   You're making the buses run on time?

Helen   I'm trying to make the buses run on time. Yes.

Nick   Fucking hell.

Helen   You see? I knew you'd do this. I knew you'd be like that.

Nick   Like what?

Helen   That you'd sneer.

Nick   Did I sneer?

Helen   Yes you did. Great big fucking sneer.

Nick   Well . . .

Helen   Well? What? What?

Nick   It's a bit petty, isn't it?

Helen   To you. Maybe to you. But if you're stuck on some shitty estate and the only way to get out, the only way to get to the shops is a bus / and at the moment there is no bus, then no it's actually very important actually.

Nick   Get to the shops? Get to the shops?

Helen   We're actually making people's lives better. What did you ever do, / Nick? What did we ever do? Sure talk, talk, talk, march, march, protest. Ban this, overthrow that, but what did we ever do?

Nick   And what about the big targets? Why are there shitty estates? Why are they there in the first place? / You should be going for the big targets.

Helen   Oh yes. Come the revolution, down they come. But while we're waiting . . .

Nick   Let's fiddle with the fucking bus timetables. / So fucking petty.

Helen *picks up* **Nick**'*s clothes.*

Helen   Tell me one concrete thing we ever did. Go on, Nick. Fuck off. Fuck off.

Nick   I'm sorry. I . . .

Helen   I don't want you here. I don't want to see you. I don't ever want to see you. Go.

Nick   Helen, I'm sorry. I didn't mean to do that. I . . .

Helen   Goodbye. There's a whole big bad world out there waiting for you. Fuck off.

Scene Two

Airport.

Nadia   Because we all have our own journeys that we're travelling. Each of us has our own path and, of course, we can't always see the path, sometimes it seems like there's no sense in anything, you know? But of course there is. Everything makes sense.

Victor   You think so?

Nadia   Oh yes, of course, yes.

Victor   I don't think so.

Nadia   No?

Victor   I think everything is crazy. The whole world is fucking crazy.

Nadia   Maybe it seems –

Victor   Yes. Everything is totally crazy. I like that. I'm a crazy person.

Nadia   No you're not.

Victor   Yeah, totally fucking crazy.

Nadia   I don't think you're crazy.

Victor   Every day I wake up and I say 'Another fucking crazy day. What am I going to do today?'

Nadia   I think you're a very beautiful person.

Victor   You like my body?

Nadia   On the inside. Beautiful on the inside.

Victor   You don't like my body?

Nadia   Of course, you've got a great body.

Victor   I've got a fucking fantastic body. I could have been in porno. Body like this I could be huge porno star. Guys go crazy for my body.

Nadia   You've had lots of partners?

Victor   Please?

Nadia   You've had a lot of boyfriends?

Victor   Boyfriends, yes. Many boyfriends. They go crazy for my body. But also my father, yes? My father and my brother go crazy for my body.

Nadia   So . . . you're close as a family?

Victor   Please?

Nadia   A very loving family.

Victor   Yes I think so. Yes. My brother he likes to
photograph me, you know? Polaroid? Since I was fourteen.
Polaroid of my body. See? (*Offers* **Nadia** *the Polaroids.*) See?
Fucking fantastic body.

Nadia   And that's your . . . ? Right. Right.

Victor   And I say to my brother when I am fourteen: I
could be in porno.

Nadia   Well that's great.

Victor   Yes?

Nadia   Yes, I think it's great to have an ambition.
Something you want and really go for it.

Victor   One day I was so fucking crazy I took Polaroids
and I . . . please word is . . . I . . . scan Polaroids on home
page and I say: 'Look at this great body. Great body, crazy
guy. Any other crazy guys out there want to do stuff with
this fucking crazy body?'

Nadia   Well I think that's fantastic. No I do. To be open.

Victor   Yes. Open. Hungry hole.

Nadia   To possibilities.

Victor   And what do you want?

Nadia   Well . . .

Victor   What are you going for?

Nadia   I don't know yet. I'm still trying to find out, you
know? Where I really belong in the universe. Nothing's
fixed for me, which is cool in a way. Sometimes you just
have to let yourself be open to possibilities before you can
really choose, you know?

Victor   When will Tim be back? I really like the idea of
Japanese guy. For one hundred days every year he will keep
me in cave.

Nadia   But you chose Tim.

Victor   I just want to be in London.

Nadia   But Tim brought you here. Tim paid for you to be here.

Victor   Everyone in London gave up on that meaning bullshit years ago, you know? And now they enjoy theirself. I love trash, okay? I like it when everything is trash. Trash music, trash food, trash people. I love these things.

Nadia   I don't think Tim is trash.

Victor   Oh yes, he told me. His home page: 'I'm one hundred per cent pure trash.'

Nadia   He may have said that . . .

Victor   And I say: 'Yes. This is the guy I want to meet. This trash guy.'

Nadia   I think Tim's self-esteem –

Victor   Please?

Nadia   I don't think Tim always values himself. But actually, Tim is a very beautiful person. A very loving person.

Victor   Oh no. This is not possible.

Nadia   Yes. A person with a lot of love to give.

Victor   Why didn't he tell me?

Nadia   Yes. And actually a very spiritual person.

Victor   He has lied to me. Fuck this. Why didn't he say?

Nadia   I don't know. Maybe he was ill and in a vulnerable position.

Victor   Ill?

Nadia   Maybe.

Victor   He is ill?

Nadia   No I don't . . .

Victor   Why does this happen to me? This always happens to me. I'm a crazy guy, you know, and I just want to have fun, just want to enjoy . . . Why do these guys fucking lie to me? Loving, spiritual, vulnerable, ill. Fuck this.

Nadia   What are you doing?

Victor   I'm going.

Nadia   But Tim isn't back yet.

Victor   I don't want to see this liar.

Nadia   Please wait for him. He'll be back with food in a minute, then we can / get the tube.

Victor   No. I don't need this.

Nadia   He wants you here. He's been looking forward to . . . It means so much / to him.

Victor   Means? Means? Fuck this 'means'. Nothing means anything, okay?

He moves to exit.

I find a guy to pay my fare out of here.

Nadia   Who?

Victor   Any guy. They're all crazy for me. Some guy will fly me to Japan and I will live in cave.

*Enter **Tim** with sweets and cherryade.*

Tim   Daddy's here. Look at this. Total crap, love it. Total fucking shite the lot of it. Not a vitamin in sight, fabulous. Lucky bag for everyone. For you.

Nadia   Thank you.

Tim   And for you.

Victor   No.

Tim   It's for you. Special trash delivery.

Victor   I don't want this.

Tim   Cherryade? Let's all have cherryade.

Victor   Fucking bastard.

Tim   Who's a . . . ?

Victor   You, you fucking bastard.

Tim   What have I . . . ?

Nadia   Please. I'm sorry.

Victor   Spiritual? She says you're spiritual.

Tim   Well she shouldn't have done that. Why do you always do this?

Nadia   I didn't know.

Tim   Just when I've met someone. Just when I'm having some fun at last.

Nadia   I just wanted him to understand / that you have feelings.

Tim   There's nothing to understand.

Victor   I'm going.

Tim   No.

Nadia   That you feel something.

Tim   No I don't. I don't feel anything, alright?

Nadia   But you do, I know you do / and I know you want someone in your life because you've got this need . . .

Tim   Don't you tell me. I want to have fun.

Nadia   And we feel the need.

Tim   Just because you're . . . Just because you've got no one.

Nadia   I've got Simon.

Tim   Yeah?

Nadia   Sometimes, yes, often I've got Simon.

Tim   And look what Simon does to you. Look at how Simon hurts / you all the time.

Nadia   No. I'm not listening to all this negative . . . No, I'm going now. I'll make my own way back. I'm going. And who knows? I might meet someone on the way back. Because I'm open, I'm at peace with myself, I don't have to . . .

Tim   What? What?

Nadia   Pay for a . . . sex . . . slave.

Nadia *exits.*

Tim   She shouldn't have said that, it isn't true.

Victor   You don't want slave?

Tim   That I feel anything, it isn't true.

Victor   So. This doesn't mean anything?

Tim   It means nothing.

Victor   And you're trash?

Tim   We're both trash. Come on, eat something, eat some rubbish.

He gets his pills out.

And Nadia's trash too really. She's alright, you'll get to like her after a bit. She's been good to me. We have fun together.

He takes the pills.

Victor   You are ill?

Tim   No.

Victor   She told me this, you are ill.

Tim No.

Victor Then what is this? This is medicine.

Tim This? This is total trash. More delicious chemical shite to fill my body with.

Victor I don't want to be near ill people. They have ugly bodies.

Tim Alright.

Victor I could be in any country in the world with any guy.

Tim But I paid for you. I own you.

Victor Please. What is it like to be ill?

Tim Are you feeling sorry for me?

Victor No.

Tim So what are you feeling?

Victor Nothing.

Tim Good boy, because I warn you, you feel anything, you're out, okay? And you pay your own way home.

Victor Okay.

Tim Come on.

He holds up a sweet.

Train in the tunnel. Chug, chug, chug.

He feeds **Victor**.

Good.

Scene Three

Nadia*'s flat.*

Dark.

Nick   Where do you wanna . . . ?

Nadia   Through here.

Enter **Nadia**, *supported by* **Nick**. *We can only see their silhouettes.*
Nadia *is wearing a knee-length coat.*

Nadia   Oh shit. Shit.

Nick   C'mon. You're alright now.

Nadia   Fuck. I feel . . .

Nick   Yeah?

Nadia   Nauseous.

Nick   Yeah?

Nadia   Like I'm gonna . . . No. No. I'm alright. I'm
alright.

Nick   Right.

Nadia *turns a light on. We can now see that her lip is cut and
swollen.*

Nadia   That's better.

Pause.

Well . . . thanks.

Nick   That's alright.

Nadia   No really, thanks. You were amazing. Just leapt in
there out of the blue like –

Nick   Yeah, well . . . I don't like to see a bloke do that to a
woman.

Nadia   Of course not.

Nick I don't like men who / don't respect . . .

Nadia Right.

Nick I can't stand that.

Nadia Of course you can't. Look. I expect you need to . . .

Nick Yeah.

Exit **Nadia** *to kitchen.* **Nick** *hesitates. Is he supposed to leave? Decides to wait. Enter* **Nadia** *with a packet of frozen food held up to her face. Doesn't see* **Nick***.*

Nick Who was he?

Nadia Oh. Hi. I'd just filed you away. In here. Past tense.

Nick Was he your boyfriend?

Nadia I don't know. / I'm fine now if you need to . . .

Nick You don't know?

Nadia I knew this would come in handy. In the fridge when I moved in. Two years ago.

Nick You don't know / if he's your boyfriend?

Nadia And I thought: It's got to be good for something. Obviously I wasn't going to eat it. I mean 'Best before December 1984', you're not going to eat it, are you?

Nick How can you not know if / he's your boyfriend?

Nadia But I thought: Hold on to it. Everything has its value. Everything is of use. Don't you agree?

Nick Who is he? A stranger?

Nadia No. Not a stranger.

Nick So? Ex-boyfriend? Ex-husband? / Pimp or . . .

Nadia Oooo . . . labels, labels. Simon's a friend who I shag once in a while. If we're in the mood.

Nick And who once in a while beats you about.

Nadia   He had a difficult childhood.

Nick   He's not making much of a go at being an adult.

Nadia   He's doing the best he can with the knowledge that he has.

Nick   Yeah?

Nadia   Yes.

She moves to the ansaphone, pushes play.

Ansaphone (female voice), 'Hi. Me returning your call returning my call returning your call returning my call. / Et cetera. And so on. Ad infinitum. So. Call me.'

Nadia (*laughs*)   Can you believe it? Three months of messages and we've never actually spoken?

Ansaphone (male voice), 'Hello sexy gorgeous sexy you. / You were gorgeous, I was gorgeous. Let's do it again.'

Nadia   Creep. Big, big mistake. I don't think so.

Pause.

Look. I'm fine now. Really, I'm okay. So if you wanna . . . you probably need to get back to your boyfriend.

Nick   No, no.

Nadia   You need to carry on looking for a boyfriend?

Nick   No.

Nadia   No?

Nick   I'm . . . y'know . . . hetero . . . straight.

Nadia   Really?

Nick   Yeah, really. I mean, don't I look like I'm . . . ?

Nadia   You look like . . .

Nick   A / convict

Nadia   A convict. You look like a convict or a poof. And since you're not a convict . . .

Nick   I'm not a poof.

Nadia   So what are you?

Nick   I was just making my way along that street . . .

Nadia   Which is a very poofy street.

Nick   To get to another street where they have a club with dancing.

Nadia   Do you like dancing?

Nick   I'm not much of a dancer.

Nadia   Bet you / could be.

Nick   I can't dance. But this club. They have like girls who dance on tables. With just little . . . things on.

Nadia   Little things?

Nick   Little . . . yes.

Nadia   Hussies.

Nick   Yeah.

Nadia   What does a nice bloke like you want with hussies like that?

Nick   Company.

Nadia   Lonely?

Nick   . . . Yeah.

Pause. **Nick** *leans in to her. Kisses her. She screams out.*

Nadia   Fuck. Fuck.

Nick   I'm sorry. I'm sorry.

Nadia   Bleeding again now.

Nick   I'm really sorry.

Nadia Stupid cunt.

*Exit **Nadia** to bathroom.*

Nick Is there anything I can . . . ?

Nadia (*off*) Yeah. Fuck off.

Nick Alright then. I'll do that. Yeah. I'll fuck off and next time Simon's beating the fucking shit out of you I won't . . . Yeah.

He starts to go. The phone rings.

Your phone's . . .

Ansaphone (male voice), 'Hey listen, I just wanted to say how profoundly sorry . . . look, I know I fucked up . . . and I really thought I'd broken this pattern of . . . I'm really trying to work though this . . . control issue or whatever it is. I'm really . . . I want to understand why I have this need to hurt you. And I want to, I need to talk about it. And I thought if I came over. Look. I know you're there. I know you're listening to this. And. I want to wash the blood away. I want to . . . I'm coming over now. I'm . . .'

Nick *picks up the phone.*

Nick Simon? . . . It doesn't matter who I am. It doesn't matter.

Nadia *enters. She has a hand mirror and a flannel for mopping up the blood.* **Nick** *doesn't see her.*

Nick (*to phone*) Because I'm a great big enormous angry bastard and I'm staying here, so don't you come anywhere fucking near her, alright? Alright?

Nick *puts the phone down.*

Nadia You're quite a frightened person, aren't you?

Nick What?

Nadia A frightened person. And you're an angry person.

Nick Well, yeah.

Nadia Yes. They're often very linked. Fear and anger. I'm a nice person.

Nick Yeah.

Nadia No. I am. Which is not such an easy thing to say. I mean I can say it now. I'm a nice person. But that's quite a new thing for me, you know?

Nick Right.

Nadia We had to practise. With a mirror.

She looks into the mirror.

I'm a nice person.

Nick I see.

Nadia I had to be given permission to do that, you know? Because before, of course, no one was giving me permission but now . . . And what about you?

She holds out the mirror.

Give it a go. If you're ready to . . . give it a go.

Nick *looks in the mirror.*

Nadia What are you thinking?

Nick I . . .

Nadia Don't censor yourself. First thing that comes into your head.

Nick Fucking old.

Nadia Yes?

Nick I think I look fucking old.

Nadia And how does that make you feel?

Nick Just . . . ancient.

Nadia You've got a great face. It's a face with character.

Nick I used to look a lot better than this.

Nadia   You are where you are.

Nick   I mean I was never Steve McQueen . . .

Nadia   Steve McQueen?

Nick   Yeah. I was never . . .

Nadia   Who's Steve McQueen?

Nick   He was . . . he must have been before your time.

Nadia   You're not trapped by your face though, are you? You're not going to let that trap you.

Nick   I've never been bothered with appearances.

Nadia   Yeah. It's what's inside that counts, isn't it? And I only have people in my life who've got really beautiful insides. Because I'm a nice person, you attract nice people, you know?

Nick   Really?

Nadia   Which is why you're here now.

Nick   Simon didn't seem like a very nice person.

Nadia   Simon's alright.

Nick   He was hitting you. And I think he would have gone on hitting you . . .

Nadia   It was good that it happened. Really. Because if Simon hadn't got frightened . . .

Nick   Frightened?

Nadia   Yeah. If Simon hadn't got frightened then I wouldn't have met you.

Nick   I don't think Simon was frightened.

Nadia   Oh he was.

Nick   I think Simon is a person who hates women. I think Simon is the sort of bastard who likes to beat up / women.

Nadia   But if you look inside . . . Simon is frightened and Simon was expressing his fear in the only way he knows how.

Nick   He cut your lip.

Nadia   I don't remember.

Nick   You must remember.

Nadia   That's in the past.

Nick   There was blood.

Nadia   Was there?

Nick   Of course there was. There was a lot of blood.

Nadia   I'm not holding on to that.

Nick   No?

Nadia   I'm letting that go. I'm not going to hurt myself by holding on to those feelings. That would be hurting me.

Nick   Maybe I'll do something. Maybe I'll kick the shit out of Simon.

Nadia   And that would hurt you.

Nick   I'm gonna do it. Where does the bastard live? Where the fuck is he?

Nadia   Hey. Hey. Hey. Easy.

Nick   You've gotta fight back.

Nadia   No.

Nick   You can't let them walk all over you.

Nadia   Them?

Nick   Men. You can't let them . . . you've got to make a stand.

Nadia   Hey. Don't generalise. Don't label people like that. 'Men'. What does that mean? 'Men'. Simon is a person.

Nick   Simon is a sexist bastard.

Nadia   He is a child inside. And we're all children inside.

Nick   I'm not. / I'm not.

Nadia   Oh, you are.

Nick   I'm a great big fucking angry adult, that's what I am. I'm someone who doesn't let the bastards get at me.

Nadia   I don't think Simon / was getting at you.

Nick   Someone who gets the bastards before they can get me.

Nadia   No one's getting at you . . . you're projecting . . .

Nick   Oh come on, come on. There's loads of them. Yeah . . . The police, the . . . multinationals . . . . The arms dealers . . . the dictators. / They're out there and you and me, we've got to stand up and . . .

Nadia *laughs.*

Nick   What? What?

Nadia   You're funny.

Nick   Funny? Funny am I?

Nadia   Yeah. All that anger. It's . . .

Nick   It's not funny, it's not . . . it's not funny when . . . because Simon is a symptom, Simon is . . . when all the time they can smack you in the mouth.

Nadia   Don't generalise . . . / don't . . .

Nick   You've got to do something, you've got to . . .

He starts shaking **Nadia** *violently.*

It's like you're sleepwalking. / You're a sleepwalker. Come on. Wake up. Wake up.

Nadia   Hey. Off. Off. Off me.

She pushes **Nick** *away.*

Pause.

Blood's starting again now. You've made the blood start again.

She applies the towel to her lip.

Pause.

Nick   Listen. I'm . . . I'm sorry.

Nadia   Yeah. Well . . .

Nick   Fuck. I'm . . .

Nick *moves to exit.*

Nadia   What are you doing? Why are you going?

Nick   Because I think I should.

Nadia   Well, don't do what you think you should . . .

Nick   I think I'm a bastard and I don't think I should be here.

Nadia   Do what you feel. What do you feel?

Nick   I don't know.

Nadia   Well, get in touch with what you feel, okay?

Nick   Okay.

Pause.

Nadia   And . . .

Nick   And . . .

Nadia   What do you feel?

Nick   I think you're really attractive.

Nadia   Thank you.

Nick   And I think I'm really attracted to you.

Nadia   Well, that's good. Because I'm really attracted to you.

Nick   Right. So . . .

Nadia   So I want you to stay. What do you want?

Nick   I want to stay.

Nadia   Okay. Then . . .

She moves to **Nick**. *They kiss.*

You gonna stay?

Nick   Yes.

Nadia *undoes her coat. Lets it drop to the floor. She is wearing table-dancing gear.*

Nadia   Is this what you meant? A little 'thing'? Is this it?

Nick   Yeah.

Nadia   I'd just finished my shift. I was on my way home. You wouldn't have got me dancing on your table. You would have got some other hussy. Who wouldn't have been as good as this hussy. Need to ring anyone?

Nick   No.

Nadia   Nobody expecting you back?

Nick   No.

Nadia   Right. Live with anyone?

Nick   No.

Nadia   So you live . . .

Nick   I'm sort of . . . I've been away for a while and so I'm in sort of temporary . . .

Nadia   I see.

Nick   Yeah. Temporary.

Nadia   Travelling? You've been away travelling?

Nick   No. Not travelling. Prison. I've been in prison. Since nineteen eighty-four.

Nadia   A convict.

Nick   I thought I'd better tell you that.

Nadia   That's cool. Are you a rapist?

Nick   No.

Nadia   That's cool. Paedophile?

Nick   Fuck. No. Do I look like a paedophile?

Nadia   I've never met a paedophile. Well, only my father. But I don't count him. So not a rapist, not a paedophile . . .

Nick   No. I . . .

Nadia   No. I'll get it . . . murderer? Attempted murder?

Nick   Well . . .

Nadia   Yeah. I'm right, aren't I?

Nick   Sort of.

Nadia   A sort of attempted murder.

Nick   I never wanted . . .

Nadia   But you've moved on. You're a changed person and . . . that's cool.

Nadia *moves to kiss* **Nick**.

Nick   You must want to find out.

Nadia   No. I don't want to know anything.

Nick   But you've got to want to know. You must want to find out . . .

Nadia   I don't want to find out anything. The past is gone, okay?

Nick   But what if I'm a psychotic / killer who wants to . . .

Nadia   I trust myself. You're a good person.

Nick   No. Let me tell you. I want / to tell you.

Nadia   It's safe. We're safe. Everything's fine. Sssshh.

They kiss. The phone rings. **Nadia** *stops* **Nick** *from picking up the phone as . . .*

Ansaphone (male voice), 'Who is he? Who the fuck is he? I know you're both there. I know you're both listening to this. So what is he you fucking slut? Where did you find him?'

Nadia   Let's go to bed.

Ansaphone, 'I hope he's a fucking serial killer you cunt. I hope he fucking slices you right open. Yeah. And boils you away.'

Scene Four

Terrace of the House of Commons.

Helen *is sitting looking at the Thames. Enter* **Jonathan**, *dressed very smartly.*

Jonathan   Marvellous, isn't it?

Helen   Mmmm.

Jonathan   Thames always stirs something, doesn't it?

Helen   Yes.

Jonathan   Are you stirred?

Helen   Oh yes, definitely stirred.

Jonathan   Are you a regular? Do you regularly take a breather from the business of Government? Take a moment to just stand here and say 'I may be a very powerful person, I may be holding the nation's destiny in my hands . . .'

Helen   No, no, no.

Jonathan   Oh yes, I know Government can do so very little nowadays. You all say that now, don't you?

Helen   No, I'm ...

Jonathan   There's the multinationals, the World Bank, NATO, Europe and there's the grass roots, there's roadshows where you listen, listen, listen, but still when all's said and done ...

Helen   No.

Jonathan   The nation's destiny in your hands. But you look at the Thames and you feel humbled, yes?

Helen   The Thames, yes. But actually, strictly day pass, I'm afraid.

Jonathan   I see, so you're ... ?

Helen   Visiting.

Jonathan   I see. Forgive me. I really did think ...

Helen   Just wanted to say I'd been on the terrace really.

Jonathan   I could have sworn I've seen you ...

Helen   No, sorry.

Jonathan   Weighed down by the burden of the office and snapped at by some media studies graduate on late-night television.

Helen   No.

Jonathan   Ah well, you have the air ...

Helen   Yes?

Jonathan   Of someone who ... Maybe some future date.

Helen   You think so?

Jonathan   Oh yes. At some future date the Party will call.

Helen   Well actually ...

Jonathan   Yes?

Helen   No, nothing.

Jonathan   Please.

Helen   There has been talk. My work . . .

Jonathan   Your work?

Helen   Yes, my work has been noticed.

Jonathan   Straightening out the single mothers? Dealing with the dealers?

Helen   I do what I can. My work in local government . . .

Jonathan   Normally so thankless.

Helen   My work's been noticed and my constituency suggested I come in for a day, shadow, get a feel for the place.

Jonathan   And how does being a shadow suit you?

Helen   Very . . . informative.

Jonathan   And inspiring?

Helen   Yes I suppose so. Yes, and inspiring.

Jonathan   Excellent. So much to sort out. So much we could do better. Someone like you . . .

Helen   I hope so.

Jonathan   Can't be far off.

Helen   And you're . . . ?

Jonathan   Another day pass.

Helen   I see.

Jonathan   Not shadowing, advising. Doing what I can. An outside eye.

Helen   Right.

Jonathan You're very curious to know what it is, aren't you? My advice, and really I shouldn't . . .

Helen I understand.

Jonathan But since you've confided in me it would / be churlish . . .

Helen No, no –

Jonathan . . . not to reciprocate. You see, the thing is, the world is going to end.

Helen *laughs*.

Jonathan Yes, I know. That's the problem, denial, it's a big problem.

Helen I'm sorry, I really didn't mean to . . .

Jonathan Denial is a major factor. But at last there are those at the top listening.

Helen I'm sorry, I said I'd be in the tea room . . .

Jonathan The big boys have accepted the possibility, then, of course, we've got to ensure that it's all managed as smoothly as possible.

Helen I promised I'd be . . .

Jonathan Can't have a wobble in the last few hours, can we? Can't have everyone going off-message and throwing us all into confusion as we reach the end.

Helen I've got to go.

Jonathan Don't you . . . Listen to me. You won't hear anything more important than this, alright? You can shadow, you can fact find, but this is . . . You listen.

Helen I really don't think / I need to hear . . .

Jonathan Because this has got to be the People's Armageddon, you see? We want to make sure that everybody has been listened to, that every social and racial

grouping is represented in the events of the last few days.
Exclusion must be avoided.

Helen   Listen. I have a sense of humour, I understand
jokes, and I've enjoyed this enormously. I'm sure tomorrow
in the middle of a very dull meeting about street lighting I
shall look back on this meeting and smile to myself, so thank
you for that.

Jonathan   Are you patronising me?

Helen   Well, yes I probably am.

Jonathan   Yes, you are and of course you're right, best
thing to do.

Helen   But now I'm going to have to get on.

Jonathan   Do you have any money?

Helen   I'm sorry?

Jonathan   Money. I'm rather hoping that you're carrying
cash.

Helen   No.

Jonathan   I really could do with an injection of capital.

Helen   No chance.

Jonathan   Thing is they send you out of rehab and what
they don't take into account is you need a good lump sum if
your dealer's even going to offer you some second-rate gear.

Helen   I don't give money to people with a drug problem.

Jonathan   I have a cash problem. My problem is I think
you've got some money and I don't want to use force to get
it from you.

Helen   That sounds very threatening.

Jonathan   I suppose it does.

Helen   Maybe I'll call security.

Jonathan   How unfortunate, 'Wannabe MP in terrace fracas'.

Helen   I think you ought to leave.

Jonathan   Alright Helen, alright then. But maybe, Helen, I could take a number . . .

Helen   No.

Jonathan   Should, Helen, I need to contact you.

Helen   I don't think so.

Jonathan   I think, Helen, it would be good if we could talk at a later date.

Helen   You're not getting any money.

Jonathan   I'm sorry, it is Helen, isn't it? Yes of course it is. Sometime pamphleteer. Sometime, a long time ago now, writer of 'A guide to destroying the rich'. Yes? Of course, yes. 'We will start with individuals. One by one we will capture them, we will capture their children. There are a thousand years of injustice to reverse. When we strike it will be with a deadly cruelty which will wipe out a thousand years of suffering.'

Helen   That was another person.

Jonathan   Of course it was. It was you but still . . .

Helen   Another person.

Jonathan   Yes.

Helen   That was . . . It was a child.

Jonathan   Of course here on the terrace, the Thames, waiting for tea. It all seems like another world. But still, when you've suffered as I've suffered. When Nick took you at your word. Followed you to the letter. When my body was beaten and scarred . . .

Helen   I'm sorry.

Jonathan   Please.

Helen   I'm so sorry for all he . . . we . . . did to you.

Jonathan   Very fashionable now, sorry, isn't it? Sorry we bombed your embassy, sorry about that famine, sorry we injected you with that virus and observed you as you died. Sorry, sorry, sorry. Well it doesn't fucking work, okay? It won't work.

Helen   Look, have some money.

Jonathan   That's very generous of you.

Helen   Please. It's the least I can . . .

Jonathan   My dealer will sleep easy in his bed for this.

Helen *hands him a ten-pound note.*

Jonathan   Ten pounds?

Helen   It's all I've got.

Jonathan   Ten pounds?

Helen   Take it.

Jonathan   No, Helen, I don't want ten pounds, Helen. Don't be so fucking stupid. I mean, do I look like a junkie? You're going to have to sort out the bullshit from the truth if you want a future in Government. Where's Nick?

Helen   I don't know.

Jonathan   Come on. He's out. Bound to head straight for you.

Helen   I don't know where he is.

Jonathan   You've got to help me. It hurts so much the past, you know? I've got to find Nick.

Scene Five

Nadia*'s flat.*

Very loud music. **Victor** *is dancing in a pair of shorts as* **Tim** *cheers him on.*

Tim   Go baby go. Go, go, go, go.

Enter **Nick**.

Nick   What the fuck?

Victor *dances around* **Nick***, bumping and grinding him.* **Nick** *tries to push him away.* **Victor** *carries on.*

Nick   Where's Nadia? Where is she?

The dancing carries on. **Nick** *grabs* **Victor** *and shakes him.*

Tell me where she is.

Victor   Craz-eeeee.

Tim *pulls* **Nick** *off* **Victor***. Pause.* **Nick** *turns off the music.*

Nick   Where's Nadia?

Tim   You must be Nick.

Nick   Tell me where she is.

Tim   I've heard about you.

Nick (*to* **Victor**)   Do you know where she is?

Tim   You won't get any sense from him.

Victor   Off my tits, yeah.

Victor *continues to gyrate in silence.*

Nick   What's wrong with him?

Tim   He's happy. Leave him alone, he's mine.

Nick   Who are you?

Tim   I'm Nadia's very best and closest friend.

Nick   Right. I can't find her. She's supposed to be back and . . .

Tim   She's supposed to be back . . . ?

Nick   Ten minutes ago.

Tim   Ten minutes?

Nick   Ten minutes, yeah, and she's not here and I was getting worried and I went to look for her and . . .

Tim   Nadia attracts people like you.

Nick   People like . . .

Tim   Obsessive people.

Nick   I'm not. I care about her. I want to look after her.

Tim   As long as you respect her space.

Nick   I want to watch her all the time.

Tim   She's her own person.

Nick   But she's her own person. Yes.

Tim   Ten minutes. Yes, obsessive and dangerous people.

Nick   I'm not. No, no.

Victor (*to* **Nick**)   You like my body?

Nick   What?

Victor   You like my body?

Tim   Tell him yes.

Nick   I think something's happened to her.

Victor   He doesn't like my body. Fucking bastard.

Tim   Upset him now. (*To* **Victor**.) Alright, baby. It's alright.

Victor   I've got a fucking fantastic body.

Tim   Easy, baby, easy.

Victor   Guys go crazy for my body.

Tim   Sit, SIT. (*To* **Nick**.) You have to be firm with them. So . . . Nineteen eighty-four. You've been away since nineteen eighty-four.

Nick   That's right.

Tim   In prison since nineteen eighty-four.

Nick   That's right.

Tim   A lot's happened since nineteen eighty-four. A lot to catch up on.

Nick   I suppose there must be.

Tim   Well my balls have dropped for a start. Nineteen eighty-eight that was. And I started shaving. Nineteen ninety.

Victor   I want the music.

Tim   I told you. (*To* **Nick**.) Bit of whizz and he keeps going for three days. (*To* **Victor**.) Wait. Daddy's talking. (*To* **Nick**.) Nadia's a good person, you know?

Nick   She's been good to me.

Tim   She really likes you. I know that for a fact because she told me. So you be good to her.

Nick   I will be.

Tim   Because we're not going to let Nadia live with a bloke who isn't good to her.

Nick   I'm doing my best.

Tim   Which is all that any of us can do.

Tim*'s beeper goes off.*

Victor   Time for the medication.

Victor *gets pills and water from his bag.*

Tim   Now these are something you won't have seen in nineteen eighty-four. These are new. You wouldn't have seen these in nineteen ninety-four.

Nick   What are they?

Tim   In nineteen eighty-four you were calling it a plague, weren't you?

Nick   I don't know.

Tim   Oh I think you were.

Victor   Yes. Gay plague. Honey. Chug, chug, chug.

Victor *feeds* **Tim** *the pill.*

Nick   Maybe the tabloids / they were always reactionary bastards . . .

Tim   In nineteen eighty-four I would have been dead in six months. Whereas now . . .

Victor   Chug, chug, chug.

Victor *feeds* **Tim** *another pill.*

Nick   You've been cured?

Tim   I can spin it out for years and years.

Victor   Maybe for ever.

Nick   That's good, isn't it?

Tim   It's fucking marvellous.

Victor   Chooo-ooo.

Another pill.

Tim   The story's got a happy ending. That's something you've got to get used to. We've reached 'They all lived happily ever after' and we've gone past it and we're still carrying on. Nobody's ever written that bit before but we're doing it. This is the happy world.

Victor   Yes, happy world.

Tim   And you're part of it now.

Victor   Welcome to happy world.

Nick   Maybe I don't see it like that.

Tim   You'll get used to it.

Nick   Maybe it's not like that. Maybe there's terrible things. Maybe there's injustices that make you angry, that make you want to protest . . . make you want to . . .

Tim   Murder?

Nick   No.

Tim   Stuff that makes you want to kill?

Nick   I'm not saying that.

Tim   Nadia told me about you.

Victor   I want to dance now.

Tim   When Daddy's finished. (*To* **Nick**.) So what are you saying? You're saying things out there make you want to kill and you've got no responsibility?

Nick   I've never said that.

Tim   We're all responsible for our own actions, okay? We don't blame other people. That's very nineteen eighty-four.

Nick   Alright.

Tim   Because it's not out there any more, alright? You can't look out there and blame, blame, blame. And I can imagine what it was like for you. Everything blocked, everything weighing you down. Communists, apartheid, finger on the nuclear button. It was frightening and you were frightened.

Nick   Don't tell me, don't you tell me . . .

Tim   I'm not telling you . . .

Nick   You child, you boy / don't you fucking tell me . . .

Tim   What do you think I'm telling you?

Nick   . . . what you don't understand. Just you keep your mouth / shut if you don't understand.

Tim   Just trying to make you see.

Nick   Keep your fucking mouth shut.

Victor   Socialist?

Tim   You going to kill me?

Nick   No.

Victor   Socialist.

Tim   Because if you want to, I think you should go / right ahead.

Nick   No.

Tim   Just let me know when you're going to / kill me, alright?

Nick   Leave it.

Tim   And I'll let you know when I'm ready to be killed.

Nick   Leave it / now. I don't want to hear this.

Tim   Because one day I might get bored with being in happy land / and then we could get together.

Nick   SHUT UP. SHUT UP. SHUT THE FUCK UP.

Pause.

Victor   You are socialist?

Nick   Yeah.

Victor   I hate socialist.

Nick   Right.

Victor   Everything falling to pieces. The buildings ugly and falling down. The shops ugly, empty. The ugly people following the rules and then mocking and complaining when they think that no one is listening. All the time you know it is rotting, but all the time 'Everything is getting better. Everything is for the best. The people are marching forward to the beat of history.' This lie. This deception. This progress. Big fucking lie.

Nick   Maybe in some countries but the / principle of socialism.

Victor   Don't tell me about my country. You know nothing.

Tim   I look at people who were around in nineteen eighty-four. And I see bitter people. I think you must have spent so much time being angry that it's left you all hard and bitter, and now there's no way for you to deal with today.

Nick   I'm coping.

Tim   Yes?

Nick   Yes. Nadia's helping me and I'm coping. I want to look after her. I didn't think I'd ever want that again. Prison, you've got to look after yourself. But now I really want to look after Nadia.

Enter **Nadia**. *Her face is bruised.*

Nadia   Hello, hello. Hey, I'm sorry. I'm sorry to keep everyone waiting. What are you up to? How about going out? I think we should go out.

Victor   Dance. / Dance.

Nadia   Yeah, let's do that. Let's go out.

Tim   Are you alright?

Nadia   I'm okay.

Victor   Part-eee.

Nick   What happened to your face?

Nadia   I'm fine now. Everything's fine.

Nick   You're not, your face.

Nadia   Let's not talk about that.

Nick   Is this Simon? Has Simon been / waiting for you outside the club?

Nadia   I'm not going to talk about it.

Nick   Come on, come on, tell me.

Tim   Look. If she doesn't want to talk about it –

Nick   She's got to talk about it.

Tim   When she's ready. When she's got the right space, she'll . . .

Nadia   Yeah. When I'm ready.

Nick   Come on, come on, this is stupid. This is . . . if he's beating you up. If the bastard is doing that, then we've got to . . .

Tim   Kill him?

Nick   Do something about it.

Tim   Get round with the axe and chop, chop, chop?

Nick   Please. Tell me what he did to you.

Nadia   No. I'm not going to do that. I'm not going to latch on to some negative. I'm not going to do that.

Tim   Come to me. Come to me and we'll kiss it better.

Nadia   Yes.

Tim (*to* **Victor**)   Sweeties. Sweeties for my little girl.

*He kisses **Nadia**'s face.*

How's that?

Nadia   Hurts a bit.

Nick   Well of course it hurts a bit.

Nadia   But it's feeling better.

Victor *feeds* **Nadia** *sweets.*

Victor   Chug, chug, chug.

Nick   I look at you. You look at me and you see bitter and ugly, alright then, but I look at you and I see . . . what is this? What are you? Nothing's connected, you're not connected with anything and you're not fighting anything.

Tim   But we're happy.

Nick   Are you?

Victor   Oh yes, happy.

Nick   And what does that mean?

Tim   It means we're content with what we've got.

Nadia   And we're at peace with ourselves.

Tim   And we take responsibility for ourselves.

Nadia   And we're our own people.

Tim   And we're not letting the world get to us.

Nick   But she's bruised, bleeding . . .

Nadia   On the outside.

Tim   Yeah, you can't just look on the outside.

Nick   And what about you?

Tim   What about me?

Nick   What about you? Inside you there's chemicals fighting virus fighting your body fighting . . .

Tim   And if I stay calm . . .

Nick   You can't stay calm all the time.

Tim   It's an addiction stress, you know?

Nadia *doubles up in pain.*

Nadia   Oh shit, oh shit, oh shit. Stomach hurts. Shit.

Nick   Here . . . show me. Where?

Nadia   Here.

Nick   Did he kick you?

Nadia   I can't remember.

Nick   Did he kick you in the stomach?

Nadia   Yes, I think he probably did.

Nick   Oh sweetheart, sweetheart.

Nick *kisses* **Nadia**. **Nadia** *pulls away.*

Nadia   Thank you. There, better now. Let's go out. Come on, everybody, let's go out. Is Victor working tonight?

Victor   Oh yes.

Nadia   Victor's working in a club. He gyrates around in a cage and he's totally wild. Aren't you, Victor?

Victor   Yes, totally wild.

Nadia   And sometimes Victor takes his shorts off and everyone goes crazy.

Victor   I've got a fantastic cock.

Tim   Victor's got a fabulous dick, baby's arm.

Nadia   It's great, Nick, you'll love it.

Nick   No thanks.

Nadia   Oh come on, Nick. Come on. You'll love it.

Nick   I'm not coming.

Nadia   Oh Nick.

Tim   If it's not Nick's thing . . .

Nadia   Nick doesn't know if it's his thing until he's tried it. He's got to give it a go. Not too many go-go dancers in prison, were there, Nick?

Tim   You don't know what they get up to in there.

Nadia   Give it a go, Nick.

Nick   Please. I can't handle this.

Nadia   Handle what?

Nick   This happy stuff.

Nadia   Nick, everyone's got a right to be happy.

Nick   Well of course.

Tim   Even you've got a right to be happy. We're giving you permission.

Victor   Yes. Happy.

Nick   But I can't do it. I can't look at you. I can't look at the bruises while he gyrates.

Nadia   Well of course you won't be looking at the bruises. That's what make-up was invented for.

Tim   Make-up, Victor.

Exit **Victor**.

Nadia   Cover up the nasty stuff. And there'll be plenty of make-up on.

Nick   But it won't make them go away.

Nadia   Out of sight.

Nick   But I'll be thinking about them. I'll be worrying about you.

Enter **Victor**.

Nadia   I don't want you to think about me. I don't want you to worry about me.

Nick   But I can't help it.

Nadia   I think Nick needs an E.

Victor   Yes. Much better than socialism.

Victor fetches an E from his bag.

Tim   That's a thing that'll be new to Nick. E. Very post eighty-four.

Victor   Everyone is the same when you take this. Everybody loves everybody. Take it.

Nick   No. I'm going.

Nadia   Going where?

Nick   I don't know. I'm leaving.

Nadia   Then we'll see you later.

Nick   No, not later. I mean I'm leaving, I'm taking my stuff and I'm going.

Nadia   You don't have to do that.

Nick   I'm leaving because I can't handle this.

Nadia   But I'm handling it.

Nick   But I love you. I've fallen in love with you but I can't see you . . . all this happening to you . . . and you're not doing anything about it . . . and me being angry all the time and you . . .

Nadia   Well, alright then.

Nick   I've got to get out. I'm sorry.

Exit **Nick**.

Victor   Weak man. Socialist. He took it seriously.

Nadia   Oh shit. Oh . . .

Victor   She's taking it seriously.

Tim   Baby, baby.

Victor   Please, not serious.

Tim   Daddy's got to / deal with this.

Nadia   Oh, oh, oh. Why is this happening?

Tim   Shit happens, you know?

Nadia   This is so shit. I love him, you know.

Tim   I know / you do, baby, I know.

Victor   Please not serious.

Enter **Nick**, *with his bag.*

Nick   Bye then.

Nadia   Bye.

Nick   You gonna say anything else?

Nadia   Nothing else to say.

Nick   Well, what do you feel?

Nadia   Too much. Lots of stuff.

Victor   Nothing, you feel nothing.

Nick   Do you love me?

Nadia   Yes.

Victor   Weak.

Nick   And I love you. Tell me about Simon.

Nadia   No.

Nick   Just tell me about tonight. He kicked you in the stomach . . .

Nadia   No.

Nick   Alright.

Exit **Nick**.

Nadia   This is starting to be a pattern, you know?

Tim   Don't say that. Victor.

Nadia   I think this is a pattern. People walking out. People abandoning me.

Tim   Hey, no. There are no patterns, okay? Make-up.

Victor *makes up* **Nadia**.

Tim   Nothing's a pattern unless you make it a pattern. Patterns are only there for people who see patterns, and people who see patterns repeat patterns. So we don't look for that. We see each day as a new day and we say 'Hello new day'. What do we say?

Nadia   Hello new day.

Tim   Good girl.

Victor *puts a wig on* **Nadia**.

Nadia   Hello new day. Hello me, hello Tim, hello Victor . . . No I can't.

Nadia *exits*.

Victor (*to* **Tim**)   You promised happy world.

Scene Six

Helen's *flat*.

Nick *holds up dry-cleaned suit*.

Nick   I did your suit.

Helen   Thanks.

Nick   Your tea's ready. You hungry?

Helen   A bit.

Nick   I thought you would be. Knew you'd be in a hurry. Big day, eh?

Helen   That's right. I've only got / twenty minutes.

Nick   Twenty minutes, I know. Your tea's ready. You hungry?

Helen   What did you do today?

Nick   You know. Cleaning. Shopping. Found a belt, keep up those trousers. You're right. She must've been a big girl. Never thought I'd find little things so fulfilling –

Helen   Nick.

Nick   You're right. The old days. Always looking at the bigger picture. Everything part of the struggle, the class war . . . Forgot the little stuff.

Helen   Nick.

Nick   Or even – yeah – despised the little stuff. Making a home. Looking after someone. But now you've let me back / I want to get that right.

Helen   I let you back because you agreed to / talk to him.

Nick   I know, I know.

Helen   So why didn't you . . . ?

Nick   Tomorrow, eh?

Helen   Fucking hell, Nick.

Nick   This is what matters, isn't it? Here. Cooking for you. Making sure you look smart for your interview. Run you a bath?

Helen   No.

Nick   Let me run you a bath.

Helen   I don't want a bath.

Nick   Can't be a sticky prospective member, can you?

Helen   I don't want your food. Don't want your bath.

Nick   Please let me take care of you.

Helen   When are you going to talk to him?

Nick   Soon. Tomorrow. I will.

Helen   You've got to meet him. I'm not having him ruining this for me.

Nick   He's not going to do that.

Helen   No.

Nick   It was me that / hurt him.

Helen   He only has to mention this to someone in the Party and I'm not going to make the approved candidates list. I'll be a 'troublemaker'.

Nick   I know.

Helen   So. Why don't you . . . ?

Nick   When I'm ready.

Helen   No. No. Not when you're ready. You're never going to be . . . now. Alright. So I'm petty. What I do is petty. I've got a petty idea of being an MP.

Nick   No / that's not –

Helen   But you don't know what it's been like. All the time you were away. Well, far as I can see, prison must have been fucking heaven compared to what it's been like out here.

Nick   You reckon?

Helen   Yes I do. Stuff we've seen. Communities disappear. Greed and fear everywhere. Start off with a society and end up with individuals fighting it out. Fucking terrible.

Nick   I know / about that.

Helen   No. You were safe. My mum. Living up here. Half the time the lift doesn't work. Which in some ways is a blessing. They stink of piss and there's needles on the floor. So she takes the stairs. Seventy-five and she's climbing fifteen flights of stairs. You don't know who's there.

Muggers. Dealers. You take your life in your hands. Year before she died she was mugged three times. That finished her off.

Nick   I'm sorry.

Helen   Everything gone. Not all at once. Not some great explosion. Not one day you can see what's happening and fight back. But so gradually you don't see it. Long, dull pain. Every now and then thinking: 'How did we get from there to here? How did we let this happen? It can't get any worse.' But it does. On and on.

Nick   But now you're / doing something . . .

Helen   And you do start to make concessions. Alright – I'll let that one go. Maybe that was an unrealistic goal. Maybe I'll have to take that on board. You can't be fighting all the time. You get so fucking weary of always being angry.

Nick   Yeah.

Helen   And now finally there's a chance to do something. Too late for anything big. Too much lost for any grand gestures. But trying to pick up the pieces. Trying to create a few possibilities for the bits of humanity that are left. I've seen those bastards fuck up the country all these years. Now I want to do something about it.

Nick   Let's get you off to your interview. Let's get you selected.

Helen   No point being interviewed. No point in being selected if it all gets taken away from me because you can't face up to your past.

Nick   Time for your tea.

Helen   When are you going to talk to him?

Nick   I . . . I can't do it. Please. Just want to look after you.

Helen   I don't need you, Nick. I've got nothing in common with you. I've cut bits out of myself. Bit by bit, another belief, another dream. I've cut them all out. I'm changed. I've grown up. I'm scarred.

Nick   You're beautiful.

Helen   Talk to him.

Nick   I'm not going to do that.

Helen   Then there's no point in this. The meal. The suit. The bath. There's no point.

Nick   If I can't take care of you, then I don't mean anything.

Helen   Then live with that. You mean nothing, alright? You're meaningless. Go.

Nick   Alright then. Yeah. Yeah. And you run around from your meetings, to your committees, to your associations. Fill up your time with all this busy, busy stuff if it makes you feel better. But don't think it means you're doing anything, alright?

Helen   I'm doing, I'm doing . . .

Nick   You're doing fuck all. Just rearranging the same old shit backwards and forwards, that's what you're doing. And you call it politics. Just as meaningless as the rest of us.

Helen   I'm doing what I can.

Nick   Maybe that's where I got it wrong. Maybe nothing means anything. Maybe that's what I was running away from. So fuck. I'll be meaningless. Yeah. I'm going and I'm gonna be totally fucking meaningless, alright?

Scene Seven

Hospital.

Tim   No.

Victor   Come on, honey . . .

Tim   No.

Victor   Honey, please . . .

Tim   I told you no.

Victor   Gotta take your pills.

Tim   Got to?

Victor   Doctor says you've got to.

Tim   And I say I don't want to.

Victor   But why? The pills are keeping you alive.

Tim   But I'm not going to take the pills.

Victor   But I want you to. I want you to take them for me.

Tim   Are you taking this seriously?

Victor   No, I'm a crazy guy.

Tim   I've told you, you take this seriously, you're out.

Victor   I can't help this . . . I feel . . . I want you to get better. I want you to be with me.

Tim   That's not why I downloaded you. I didn't download you because of that. I downloaded you because you wear little shorts and you gyrate to trash. Because you are trash.

Victor   I like trash.

Tim   You like me because I'm trash.

Victor   This is different. This is caring about you and wanting you to . . . please. Come on. Please. In my country –

Tim   Which I paid for you to leave.

Victor   I know.

Tim   Which you say you're never going back to.

Victor   In my country which I'm never going back to.

Tim   Because they don't make trash like we make trash.

Victor   In my country, you would not have this medicine. Sure, if you were boyfriend of mafia-boss then mafia-boss would pay for medicine. But if you were boyfriend of go-go dancer . . .

Tim   If they had go-go dancers.

Victor   There are plenty of go-go dancers now. More go-go dancers than factory workers. Nobody ever pays factory workers. So, if you can go-go, you go-go. But if you were boyfriend of go-go dancer then this medicine would cost . . . go-go dancer dances for ten years to pay for one year of this medicine.

Tim   I'd get through an army of go-gos.

Victor   So, this medicine is no solution for people in my country. And this is worse. This is much worse. To know there is something that could save them but which they can't have.

Tim   I don't . . . I envy, you know . . .

Enter **Nadia**.

Nadia   Hello.

Tim   How did you know I was here?

Nadia   Well, Victor told me. I came straight over.

Tim   Why did you do that?

Victor   I was upset. Nadia called when I was upset and I told Nadia.

Tim   I didn't want you to tell anyone.

Victor   I know that.

Nadia   I wanted to be here. I wanted to see you.

Tim   But I don't want you to see me like this.

Nadia   It's alright.

Tim   I don't want people to see me ill.

Victor   Then take your pills.

Tim   Fuck off. Fuck off.

Victor   He won't take his pills.

Nadia   That's not right.

Victor   Make him take his pills.

Nadia   Why aren't you taking your pills?

Tim   Because I don't want to.

Nadia   But you're doing so well. They're brilliant these pills. They're what you've been waiting for. This is . . . this is a happy ending. You told me that. So . . .

Tim   I hate it. I hate being well. I can't do it.

Nadia   You feel you don't have a right to be happy.

Tim   I don't want to hear all that stuff. All that stuff we keep telling ourselves. I'm happy, you're happy. We're okay. I don't want to hear it.

Nadia   So, what? All the old stuff people used to programme themselves with – I'm a victim, I'm poor. Same old patterns?

Tim   I don't know. I envy people who can't get medicine.

Nadia   Come on.

Victor   Then you are very stupid.

Tim   Don't speak to me like that, you trash, you slave / you Russian doll.

Victor   Stupid, stupid.

Nadia   Take the pills. Please. I love you. Victor loves you. Don't you, Victor?

Tim   No he doesn't. / Just leave both of you. Go. Go.

Nadia   Victor, tell him what you feel.

Victor   No.

Nadia   You told me you were upset and you told me that you really care about Tim.

Victor   All I can think about is you. I think about you all the time. I wish I didn't feel this way but I do. I hope . . . I think. Let the trash music take it away, let the trash . . . the dumdumdum . . . let it fill up your head. Dumdum. But I can't do that any more. And I can't hear the music any more.

Tim   Maybe it's not loud enough.

Victor   I want you to be alive.

Tim   For your sake?

Victor   I want you to take them for me. For my sake.

Tim   Weak. You're a weak person. What's a person? What's a death? Millions of people out there. Millions of people out there to fuck and dance with and be with – so don't be so fucking weak. Get out there – dum, dum, dum. Because I don't want you here and I don't want to be alive.

Nadia   But being alive is great.

Tim   And what's so great about your life? Nothing. Nick's left you. Everyone's left you. You'll never hold on to anyone.

Nadia   But I've learnt from that / I've grown. I have.

Tim   Shite. Shite. Shite. You deserve each other. Cling together, you little weak people.

Victor   Yes, maybe we do that. Come. Come.

He begins to caress **Nadia**.

Come on. Feel me. I have a good body. Better than Nick, I think, yes? Better than Simon. I like women. I'm not afraid of women. I can fuck women.

Nadia *touches* **Victor**'s *body*.

Victor   How does this feel?

Nadia   Good.

Victor   You could fuck this body?

Nadia   Maybe.

Tim   Go on – fuck each other.

Victor   Yes. Fuck these gays, yes? Scared of the woman's bodies.

Nadia   Yes. Scared.

Tim   If that'll stop you being lonely, fuck each other.

Victor *and* **Nadia** *dance suggestively together*.

Victor   Gays are . . .

Nadia   Ill.

Victor   Ill and . . .

Nadia   Frightened. Frightened people.

Tim   Are you enjoying that?

Victor   I want your pussy.

Victor *goes down on* **Nadia**.

Tim   Happy now?

Victor   Sorry. You speak to . . . ?

Tim   Is that fun?

Victor   Very much. We're having fun.

Tim   My hospital room. My illness. My body. My death. My choice.

He takes the pills.

Nadia   Well done.

Victor   Thank you, honey. Thank you.

He kisses **Tim**. **Tim** *cries*. **Victor** *holds* **Tim**.

Come on, honey. Come on.

Nadia   Alright darling, alright.

Tim   I didn't want to do that. Why did you make me do that?

Victor   Please, honey . . .

Tim   This is . . . I can't stand this.

Nadia   You've done the right thing and you're alright.

Tim   I want communists and apartheid. I want the finger on the nuclear trigger. I want the gay plague.

Victor   Honey . . .

Tim   I want to know where I am. Since I was nineteen, I've known that, you know? I knew where everything was heading. And sure, it was a fucking tragedy. My life was a tragedy and that was frightening and sad and it used to do my head in. But I knew where everything was going. Bit by bit my immune system would break down until . . . no fixed figure. Five years, ten years, some amazing freaks even took fifteen years.

Victor   Honey.

Tim   And you could imagine each step before it happened because you were told what it would be. You start off feeling completely knackered.

Nadia   Darling.

Tim   Oh yes, that's happened to me. Now, I've started feeling completely knackered. I've reached the first step. Now I'm on the same path as the others. Better start resting. Wait until stage two. Skin problems. Dry skin, warts. Short of breath. Waiting until . . . lesions. Here they are. This thing is taking its course. We're moving forward. And now you can see everything all the way down the line.

Nadia   Darling.

Tim   Of course, you can't say exactly when. You can't announce a date. You can't choose the hospital. But you control what you can. And you can even imagine the funeral. You can get a clear picture of it. What people will feel, what they'll say to each other. How all the people who liked you will say nice things and how all the people who never liked you will say the same nice things. I used to know everything and that's what those fucking pills have taken away from me.

Victor   So, get used to it.

Tim   I am trying.

Victor   You get used to it and you find a way of carrying on.

Tim   What way?

Nadia   It's over now, come on, come home. Let's find a doctor and tell them we're taking you home.

Nadia *exits.*

Victor   I can't be with you if you don't take the pills.

Tim   Alright then.

Victor   You stay with me and you take the pills?

Tim   I don't know.

Victor   You've got to promise me you'll take the pills.

Tim   I can't do that.

Scene Eight

Street.

Jonathan *is washing blood away from* **Nadia**'s *face.*

Jonathan   Yes. Yes. You're going to be alright.

Nadia   Hurts so much.

Jonathan   There's a lot of blood, but actually the wound . . . the wound is pretty superficial.

Nadia   Right.

Jonathan   You're not actually disfigured.

Nadia   Well, that's good.

Jonathan   Just incredibly bloody.

Nadia   Thank God you were there.

Jonathan   I was passing. Couldn't just walk past and see a woman being attacked like that. Although now of course so many do.

Nadia   It was very . . . noble.

Jonathan   It was human nature.

Nadia   You're quite a strong person, aren't you?

Jonathan   Do you think so?

Nadia   Spiritually. And you're quite a powerful person, aren't you?

Jonathan   None of us really has any power, do we?

Nadia   You're at ease with your authority. That's very attractive. It's an attractive quality.

Jonathan   Well, thank you. Are you going to be alright?

Nadia   I don't know.

Jonathan   If I leave you now, are you going to be alright?

Nadia   You're going to abandon me?

Jonathan   I'm going to leave you. There must be someone. Who could look after you?

Nadia   Well, no actually, no. There's nobody.

Jonathan   All alone in the world?

Nadia   All alone in the world.

Jonathan   But surely . . . a friend.

Nadia   Yes. A friend. I have a friend. But he's very ill. He's in the hospital. So I look after him. So he can't look after me when Simon . . .

Jonathan   Simon?

Nadia   When Simon attacks me. When Simon gets frightened.

Jonathan   You don't believe Simon gets frightened. You don't really believe that, do you?

Nadia   Well no. Not any more. Simon . . .

Jonathan   Yes, come on, find the word.

Nadia   Hates me. Loves me in a hating kind of way. Hates me in a loving kind of way. Something. Hates me.

Jonathan   And do you love Simon?

Nadia   No.

Jonathan   But you love someone else.

Nadia   No.

Jonathan   You're lying to me. Goodbye.

Nadia   No, please. I don't want to be alone. Please.

Jonathan   I can't stand a liar. If there's one thing I can't stand it's an untruth.

Nadia   Do you want to go to bed with me? I've got a great body. And I bet you've got a great body too.

Jonathan   I'm not really interested in bodies.

Nadia   Everyone's interested in bodies.

Jonathan   Maybe there's something unnatural about me.

Nadia   Everyone's interested in my body. Men pay just for a few minutes near my body. Even when they're not allowed to touch.

She takes off her top.

What do you feel?

Jonathan   Nothing.

Nadia *begins to dance.*

Nadia   You must be feeling something now?

Jonathan   It doesn't mean anything to me. You're a very powerless person, aren't you?

Nadia   Am I?

Jonathan   Oh yes. You are a very powerless, lonely, unfocused person, aren't you?

Nadia   No. No.

Jonathan   Lying to me.

Nadia   There's a path. I've chosen a path and every thought is creating my future.

Jonathan   Lies. Lies. Lies.

Nadia   And if I can just look at the world in a positive way –

Jonathan   Deceiving me. Deceiving yourself. / Please just be honest.

Nadia   I . . . I . . . I . . .

Jonathan   Find the words. Think before you speak. Don't just mouth . . . speak.

Nadia   Everything is terrible. Nothing means anything. There's nobody out there. I'm alone in the universe.

Jonathan   Excellent. Excellent. How do you feel?

Nadia   Dead.

Jonathan   Yes. That's normal.

Nadia   It's horrible.

Jonathan   For a while you think: 'I'm dead.' But then you pass through that and . . . something else emerges.

Nadia   What? What?

Jonathan   I really think you have to discover that for yourself.

Nadia   Tell me.

Jonathan   We each have to learn for ourselves.

Nadia   Tell me. Tell me. You can't just fucking leave me to . . . Sorry. Sorry. Please. Tell me.

Jonathan   Since you insist. It won't mean anything until you actually live it.

Nadia   Alright.

Jonathan   You're dead and then you come through that and you embrace the chaos . . . you see the beauty of . . . the way money flows, the way it moves around the world faster and faster. Every second a new opportunity, every second a new disaster. The endless beginnings, the infinite endings. And each of us swept along by the great tides and winds of the markets. Is there anything more thrilling, more exhilarating than that?

Nadia   I . . .

Jonathan   Do you understand?

Nadia   Yes.

Jonathan   The truth.

Nadia   No.

Jonathan   No. But you're learning. Who are you in love with?

Nadia   It doesn't matter.

Jonathan   Tell me who it is. It's Nick, isn't it?

Nadia   What?

Jonathan   You're in love with Nick.

Nadia   You know Nick?

Jonathan   Yes. Yes.

He takes off his shirt.

These are the scars, you see? This is what Nick did to my body. This is why Nick was in prison. Where is he?

Nadia   I don't know.

Jonathan   I want to find him. Where is he?

Nadia   I don't know. The truth.

Jonathan   My body is disgusting.

Nadia   I'll kiss it better.

Jonathan   Don't be so fucking stupid. That's not going to work, is it?

Scene Nine

Hospital.

Tim *lying in a bed.*

Victor   They give us an hour. Before he's taken away.

Nadia   Yes.

Victor   So we . . . what do you want to do?

Nadia   I don't know.

Victor   I wish we knew what to do. I think maybe inside us, if we were allowed feelings we would know what to do.

Nadia   I don't think so.

Victor   Oh yes. Inside us there must be some . . .
something we should do now. Get in touch with our
feelings.

Nadia   No. I don't believe that any more.

Victor   Maybe it's fall to our knees, sway, beat our chests.
Maybe wash his body. Maybe that's inside us.

Nadia   Maybe you just saw that in a film somewhere.
There is nothing for us to do.

Victor   But we have to say goodbye.

Nadia   He's not going to hear that.

Victor   No.

He prods **Tim**.

Nothing.

Nadia   But maybe if you were alone with him. So if we
take it in turns. I'll wait outside for a while.

Nadia *exits.*

Long pause. **Victor** *looks at the body.*

Victor   Fucking stupid. Fucking.

He hits **Tim**'s *body.*

Fucking selfish fucking bastard. What about me? Make me
suffer like this. This is not what you were supposed to do.
Supposed to make me happy. Not make me suffer. I don't
want to feel this. Fuck. Fuck.

He hits the body. Several more times. Moves away.

Tim   Well, I don't think that's going to get you anywhere
is it?

Victor   It's what I feel.

Tim   Even Lazarus didn't respond well to fists.

Victor   I'm not talking to you fucking bastard.

Tim   And I certainly ain't a-coming back just because you get butch on me.

Victor   Don't want you back.

Tim   Not even a little bit?

Victor   I don't want some fucking bastard who can't even take his fucking pills.

Tim   I didn't want to live.

Victor   But I wanted –

Tim   Fuck that. I wasn't going to be miserable just so you wouldn't feel alone.

Victor   I'm not going to be alone. I find someone. Someone healthy. Someone who wants to live.

Tim   Yeah?

Victor   Yes. Wasted my time with you when I could have been with someone else.

Tim   Well go on then. Fuck off out of here. Start looking now. Good place to start. Doctors. Nurses. Porters.

Victor   No.

Tim   I don't want you in here disturbing my eternal fucking rest.

Victor   You'll be gone in an hour. Wheeled away. Into the morgue.

Tim   Which is where I want to be.

Victor   Then good. Good. Fuck. I love you.

Tim   I know you do.

Victor   Please say you love me. I don't care whether it's true or not. I don't care whether you are lying to me. Please. I just want you to say it.

Tim   You don't care if it's true?

Victor   A lie is okay. So long as I hear it.

Tim   That's . . . pathetic.

Victor   I know.

Tim   I love you.

Victor   Thank you.

Tim   When you . . . I don't know if this is just me . . . I know when you're hanged you're supposed to . . . but I've . . . maybe it's rigor mortis or . . . but I've . . . come here.

Victor   No.

Tim   Don't be disgusted. I know I must be disgusting.

Victor   It's not that. I loved you. You could never be disgusting to me.

Tim   So don't give up on me now, baby. Touch my face. Please. There. How does it feel?

Victor   Cold.

Tim   I thought it would do. Touch my heart. And now? What do you feel now?

Victor   Colder. No heart beat.

Tim   Only to be expected. Listen. I want to say sorry. I wish I could have kept going for you. I wish I could have done that. But I didn't know who I was any more. Suddenly I was nobody. When you're 'Person Who Is Dying' and they take that away from you then you're 'Person Who . . . Blank, Blank, Blank.' Nadia talks a load of bollocks, doesn't she?

Victor   Nadia loves you also.

Tim   Yes. I suppose she does. Move your hand down.

Victor   No. I can't.

Tim   Please. Please.

Victor   I'm frightened.

Tim   Don't be frightened.

Victor   And also disgusted.

Tim   Well, of course you're disgusted. But you love me.

Victor   Yes.

Tim   And I think we're allowed one final request.

Victor   Alright.

Victor's *hand moves under the sheet and on to* **Tim**'s *erection.*

Tim   Does that feel nice?

Victor   Yes.

Tim   Why do you think that's nice? I think you're sick. Twisted. Touching up a corpse.

Victor   It's nice because it means you . . .

Tim   What? What?

Victor   You want me.

Tim   Yes.

Victor   And maybe you love me.

Tim   No. I don't think it ever meant that.

Victor   No?

Tim   Maybe I need you or I need someone. To stop me being alone. Alone with this. (*Indicates his erection.*) But don't confuse that with love.

Victor   So what is love?

Tim   I never found out.

Victor   You never loved me?

Tim   I don't know if I ever loved you because I never knew what love was.

Victor   Fuck you.

Tim   No point me lying now, baby. Might as well get it all out in the open before I hit the morgue.

Victor   I want you to lie to me. Please. Make this like an opera. Sing to me. I hold you in my arms and tell me you will love me for ever.

Tim   I can't do that. Play with me.

Victor   No.

Tim   Make me come. This is real. Make me come.

Victor   It's terrible.

Tim   It's what I want.

Victor *starts to masturbate* **Tim**, *crying as he does.*

Victor   This is so shit. I hate this. Is this all there is?

Tim   That's it. Yes.

Victor   There's got to be more than this. What is there? This is . . . animals. What makes us better than animals? Revolution never saved us. Money never saved us. No love. I want more than this.

Tim   Faster. Faster.

Victor   What is it? Children? To have a child? Is that what save us? I can't have a child. Fuck this gay. Fuck these men and their fucking together.

Tim   That's good. You're good. I love you. I love you.

Victor   You only say that when I do this.

Tim   Oh yes.

Victor   Why can't you say that some other time?

Victor *pulls away.*

Tim   Don't stop.

Victor   Why do you only say 'I love you' when you feel orgasm coming?

Tim   That's when I feel like saying it.

Victor   Just one time.

Tim   Fuck you. Don't leave me like this. Finish me off. Finish it.

Victor   No.

*Enter **Nadia**. She can't hear **Tim** when he speaks.*

Nadia   How are you?

Victor   Okay.

Nadia   Did you know what to do?

Victor   I guess. I will leave you now.

*Exit **Victor**. **Nadia** sits.*

Nadia   Well . . . goodbye. I . . . goodbye.

Tim   Can you hear me?

Pause.

Please. Try to hear me.

Nadia   You were like a brother. I just want to say that.

Tim   Bring him back. I didn't mean that. I didn't want to hurt him.

Nadia   So, now I'm alone. That's what I've always been scared of. Being on my own. I'm talking, talking to someone and the words don't matter. Because what I'm really saying is . . . don't leave the room. Don't walk out. Don't leave me on my own.

Tim   Yes. Don't want to be alone now.

Nadia   Anything to be with someone. You want my body? Fine. Just stay with me a few hours. And Simon? Simon's hitting me. But I'm with someone. Bleeding but somebody's there.

Tim   Got to love someone before I'm buried.

Nadia   Well, I've learnt from this. I'm going to be on my own and I'm going to learn to do that. Hours of . . . days of . . . no one else.

Tim   I'll follow him. I'll stalk him. I'll haunt him.

Nadia   Goodbye. Goodbye.

Tim   I love him.

Scene Ten

Club.

Nick *is sitting.*

Nick   Hello.

Victor   Hello, Mr Socialist.

Nick   You dancing tonight?

Victor   No. I'm not dancing any more.

Nick   I wanna watch you dance.

Victor   I stop dancing. I come to get my money. Yes – my money and my clothes. You look terrible.

Nick   Yeah.

Victor   Please. What has happened to you?

Nick   I can't remember.

Victor   You must remember.

Nick   No. I don't remember anything. I've been drinking.

Victor   Socialist always drink.

Nick   You think so?

Victor   In my country. Yes. Man is rational being, they say. Society must be organised in rational way, they say. And they drink one bottle of vodka every day until they fall on the floor. This is you.

Nick   I've been drinking. But I'm not a socialist.

Victor   You told me.

Nick   Yeah, well. I changed my mind.

Victor   Good boy.

Nick   I thought you'd tell me where Nadia is.

Victor   I don't know.

Nick   Please. You've got to help me. I want to see her. Make things alright. I want to be part of Happy World.

Victor   Happy World?

Nick   Yeah. Every day is a new day. Take responsibility for ourselves. Not let the world get to us.

Victor   Fuck this Happy World, okay? Big fucking lie.

Nick   But you told me.

Victor   Yes. Well I changed my mind. You must forget this Nadia.

Nick   I can't.

Victor   The past is the past. You cannot go back to someone. You are with someone for a time but then you leave this person and you move on.

Nick   But I can't keep on leaving people. I can't always be moving.

Victor   Yes. This is the only thing you can do.

Nick   Just stay with somebody and do what you can to look after them.

Victor   Forget them. They are the past. Move away. You can be anywhere in the world. The world is not so big, you know? There's the same music, the same burgers, the same people. Everywhere in the world. You can keep moving all the time and still be in the same place.

Nick   I want a place I can be. Ignore the world. Look after someone I love. I want a home.

Victor   And what is this home? Nothing is fixed any more. You cannot say 'this is home'.

Helen *enters.*

Victor   You have to keep moving. Yes. This is what I will do. This is what you should do.

Helen   Nick. God, you look terrible. What happened to you? (*To* **Victor**.) What happened to him?

Victor   Socialist. Drinker.

Victor *exits.*

Nick   Meaningless, yeah? Well, this is meaningless, alright? Drinking and begging and sleeping in piss in doorways. This is what I am now. And I don't want to be saved.

Helen   I'm not here to save you.

Nick   Well, good.

Helen   You've got to talk to him, Nick. He's had you followed. He's threatening to go to the press. He's asked / me to talk to you.

Nick   I don't want to see you. I'm looking for Nadia.

Helen   Nadia?

Nick   Yeah, Nadia.

Helen   Nadia is . . .

Nick   Someone I've got attached to . . .

Helen   I see. And who is this Nadia? I thought you were attached to me.

Nick   Well yeah . . .

Helen   But – what? – now you've moved on.

Nick   I suppose that's right. Yes.

Helen   And you expect me to deal with him on my own? This is an important time for me. This is your crap and you're going to have to deal with it.

Nick   I can't.

Helen   If you hadn't done this to him in the first place . . .

Nick   I've got to forget that now. I've got to let it go.

Helen   Let it go?

Nick   Yeah. If I'm going to change and . . . change and grow as a person then I've got to let all that go.

Helen   When did you start talking like that? Is this Nadia? Does Nadia talk like this?

Enter **Nadia**.

Nadia   Hello, Nick.

Nick   Sweetheart.

Nadia   I'm looking for Victor.

Nick   You've been crying.

Nadia   Yes. Tim died this morning.

Nick   I'm sorry. Victor didn't say.

Nadia   He's here?

Helen   You must be / Nadia.

Nick   Nadia, this is Helen.

Nadia   Right. I've heard about you.

Helen   Well good.

Nadia   I didn't realise you were still around.

Helen   I pop up from time to time.

Nadia *cries*.

Nick (*to* **Helen**)   I think you ought to go now.

Helen   I'm not going.

Nick   Nadia's lost a friend.

Helen   And I'm sorry about that. But you're not leaving me / to deal with this.

Nick *moves to hold* **Nadia**.

Nick   Go on. Nadia needs me. Don't you, sweetheart?

Nadia   I think you should go to her.

Helen   I don't want that.

Nadia   Helen wants you, don't you, Helen?

Helen   I want . . . what I want is for Nick to stop running away.

Nadia   Go to her. Go to Helen.

Exit **Nadia**.

Helen   I think Nadia's letting you go.

Nick   She's upset.

Helen   I think she's changing and growing and letting you go.

Nick   Fuck off out of here.

Helen   Alright then. Alright. Ruined everything. With your gestures. Your anger. So, leave me to live with that. And you see if you can hold on to Nadia. But it looks to me like Nadia is a child and I don't think she's going to want you for very much longer. But hey – it could be fun for a while. So change and grow – you cunt.

Exit **Helen**. *Enter* **Victor** *followed by* **Nadia**.

Nadia   Victor. Please. Where did you go – just ran away?

Victor   No.

Nadia   You disappeared.

Victor   I think London is a shitty place. I think it is time for me to move on. And I think Tokyo is much better. Absolutely fucking crazy.

Nadia   If that's what you want.

Victor   Yes. I think I will be model in Tokyo and I will have my own TV show. And one day I will take many drugs and die in the snow in the mountains. I get my money.

Victor *exits*.

Nick   Sweetheart.

Nadia   You're still there. I'd wiped you out. Past tense.

Nick   Please. I love you.

Nadia   And what does that mean, Nick? It means you want to stay because all the other stuff in your life is too frightening.

Nick   No.

Nadia   Because all the stuff out there is frightening and if you say 'I'm in love with you' then it'll be like a charm and all the nasty stuff won't get to you.

Nick   You reckon?

Nadia   I'm letting you go.

Nick   Letting me go so you can move on and change and grow as a person?

Nadia   No. I don't need the bullshit. And I don't need you any more. What I want is to be on my own. Anything else is just running away. Deal with the nasty stuff, okay? I saw what you did. To that man.

Nick   Which . . .

Nadia   To that man's body. Deep scars. I felt so sorry for him, I would have slept with him.

Nick   And what did you . . . ?

Nadia   You must talk to him.

Nick   And if I did . . . would you . . .

Nadia   No. I don't want you back. Don't do it for that. Do it.

Nick   Yes.

Nadia   You're going to talk to him?

Nick   Yes. There's nothing left. I'm going to talk to him.

Enter **Victor.**

Nadia   Good.

Victor   Bye, Mr Socialist.

Exit **Nick**.

Victor   I go to airport. Find a guy to take me to Japan.

Nadia   I'll miss you.

Victor   No. You forget me tomorrow. Close your eyes and you won't be able to picture this face.

Nadia   I will.

Victor   You want to take Polaroid?

Nadia   Yes.

Victor *produces a Polaroid camera from his bag. Poses for* **Nadia**. *Enter* **Tim**.

Tim   Baby. I want you. I got frightened. Angry because I was ill, but I'm free now. Dead and free and I can tell you what I feel. I love you, baby.

Victor   I will forget you.

Nadia   No, Victor.

Tim   I won't let you. I'll be with you wherever you go. Face on a Tamagotchi. Tourist in a kimono. I'll be there.

Victor   No. I'll cut it out of me.

Nadia   I'll remember. I want to remember.

Nadia *takes the Polaroid.*

Tim   You'll be sleeping in your tiny room in Japan. An earthquake will begin. You'll be holding to your bed. Shaking. Shaking. The building will collapse. No food. No water for three days. Voices will call from the rubble in Japanese. You're going to thank fuck I'm there.

Nadia   Here we are. Starting to develop now. I can see Tim. Can you see Tim? Is he still there?

Victor   Of course not. You are crazy.

Tim   That's not true. He's lying.

Victor   You see a dead man?

Nadia   He's gone away now. Nothing. There. Something to remember you by.

Scene Eleven

Boardroom.

Nick *waits. Enter* **Jonathan**.

Jonathan   Hello. I thought it was you. Security guard said: 'He's a madman. Or a drunk. Mad drunk. We'll throw him out. Or call the police.' And I said: 'No. I think I know who it is. Send him up.'

Nick   You've been looking for me.

Jonathan   Yes.

Nick   You've been threatening people.

Jonathan   I've been persistent.

Nick   Threatening people close to me.

Jonathan   I wanted to find you.

Nick   Why?

Jonathan   I think . . . to hurt you. Punish you. I think that's what I want.

Nick   I deserve that. Here I am. What are you going to do?

Jonathan   I'd imagined someone stronger.

Nick   Come on. Come on.

Jonathan   I'd imagined someone angry and threatening and . . .

Nick   It's not a trick. Look at me. I'm not gonna fight back.

Jonathan   And someone worth fighting. And I'm looking at someone . . . weak. Lost.

Nick   Empty. I feel empty.

Jonathan   Yes. I think the world's rather done the job for me.

Nick   You can't really get much lower, can you? There's not much of me left.

Jonathan   Pretty terrible place, the world, isn't it? When you actually have to live in it.

Nick   Horrible.

Jonathan   All that confusion. All those people buzzing around hurting each other.

Nick   But you get used to it.

Jonathan   Exactly – you get used to it.

Nick   I found myself thinking: Fuck, I wish I was inside again. Last few days. I've been standing there. Watching police cars. Hanging around parked cars when there's police around. Setting off the alarms. Wah wah wah. Come on please. Put me away. One of you has got to save me.

Jonathan   And . . . ?

Nick   Nothing.

Jonathan   Where's a policeman when you need one, eh?

Nick   That's right.

Jonathan   It's good to see you.

Nick   Yeah?

Jonathan   Now that you're here, it's rather nice.

Nick   Thanks.

Jonathan   And me? Are you . . . ?

Nick   Yeah. Pleased to see you.

Jonathan   Nostalgia's a tricky bitch, isn't she? But really now, just at the moment, I feel rather nostalgic about the time we spent together.

Nick   I came to say sorry.

Jonathan   There's no need for that. You look terrible. Would you like to take a shower? We've got a splendid shower just through here.

Nick   I'm alright.

Jonathan   Maybe later. And then how about some clean clothes?

Nick I don't think so.

Jonathan I can send the girl out. It's not a problem. She enjoys shopping for me. The offer's there.

Nick It was much easier. Before. When I hated you. I knew where I stood.

Jonathan I know. You know the territory and then suddenly . . .

Nick Lost.

Jonathan Horrible, isn't it?

Nick Wish I had the strength left to hate you.

Jonathan I think we both miss the struggle. It's all been rather easy for me these last few years. And I start to feel guilty if things come too easily. But really money, capitalism if you like, is the closest we've come to the way that people actually live. And, sure, we can work out all sorts of other schemes, try and plan to make everything better. But ultimately the market is the only thing sensitive enough, flexible enough to actually respond to the way we tick.

Nick There's nothing better?

Jonathan Maybe in a thousand years but for now . . .

Nick It's the best we've got.

Jonathan Exactly. So. You can spend your time like Helen. Rush around, regulate a bit. Soften the blow for a few of the losers. All very necessary. Important work. Absolutely. But rather dull. I think it's made Helen rather . . .

Nick Dull. Yeah.

Jonathan Or you can say hey-ho – this is the way things are. So let's get in there and make the most of it. How about that shower?

Nick Alright. Thanks.

Exit **Jonathan**. **Nick** *starts to undress. Sound of shower starting. Enter* **Jonathan** *with towel.*

Jonathan   Warming up nicely. New clothes and you'll feel much better.

Nick *finishes undressing, wraps himself in the towel.*

Jonathan   Maybe you'd like to join me this afternoon. I'm making a trip. Eastern Europe. I've got a foundation. We're doing some fantastic things. I had rather a run on currencies a few years ago. Governments were behaving in a spectacularly stupid fashion. Western governments. And I made the most ridiculous amounts of money. So, I'm doing what I can in Eastern Europe. Schools and hospitals and rehab centres. We're really doing things. Oh – little flash of hatred in your eyes.

Nick   No.

Jonathan   Yes. Just for a moment – a flash of the old hatred.

Nick   I don't think so.

Jonathan   Please. There's no need to lie. You felt . . .

Nick   Yeah. You cunt.

Jonathan   Schools and hospitals and . . . but still . . .

Nick   You cunt.

Jonathan   Why do you think that is?

Nick   I don't know.

Jonathan   Don't worry. You're not alone. That's what it's like out there. I fly in to some orphanage, or college, or festival of new plays and they treat me like god – a demi-god – thank you, thank you, thank you – but still: that little flash of hatred in all of them. And I don't quite now why that is. But I rather like it. Time for your shower. Then, if you feel like it, you can come with me and look at all the good work.

Nick   I don't think so.

Jonathan   Think about it.

Scene Twelve

Helen's *flat.*

Enter **Helen**. *She wears a rosette. Hunts for leaflets. Finds them. Enter* **Nick** *from shower.*

Helen   I forgot these. What do you think? (*Shows him photo on leaflet.*)

Nick   Terrific.

Helen   How do I look? Suitably middle-aged?

Nick   Yeah. No. You're getting my vote.

Helen   Good. Shall we send a car round? Get you to the polling station.

Nick   It's alright.

Helen   It's pissing with rain.

Nick   I don't mind a bit of rain.

Helen   My hero.

Helen *moves to exit.*

Nick   Thanks for having me back.

Helen   Still time to change the locks, eh?

Nick   Course. Why did you take me back?

Helen   I'm all heart.

Nick   Why?

Helen   I don't . . . Maybe because I can't always wake up and think: let's manage this, let's organise that. Because sometimes I think . . .

Nick Yeah?

Helen This is all wrong. I want to change everything. I want to smash everything up.

Nick You think that?

Helen Sometimes. Just for a moment after I've woken up and then I think: no. Get on with the day. Do what I can.

Nick That's what grown-ups think.

Helen Yeah. That's what grown-ups think.

Nick We're old, aren't we?

Helen Fucking old. But you . . . I want you to be angry.

Nick I can't do that any more.

Helen Nobody does that any more. I miss that.

Nick I can't be your memory.

Helen I want to make you into what you used to be.

Nick That's going to be difficult.

Helen Well I'm going to have a fucking good try.

Nick Just you try.

He moves to kiss her.

Helen I'm damp.

Nick So am I.

They kiss.

For a complete catalogue of Methuen Drama titles
write to:

Methuen Drama
11–12 Buckingham Gate,
London SW1E 6LB

or you can visit our website at:

www.methuen.co.uk